Holding the Earth Together

Holding the Earth Together

Youth Voices Speak For Our World

Poetry and Art by the Students of the Stories of Arrival Refugee and Immigrant Poetry Project

Edited by
MERNA ANN HECHT

Introduced by
MERNA ANN HECHT
CARRIE STRADLEY

CHATWIN BOOKS

2018

Stories of Arrival: Youth Voices Poetry Project
Merna Ann Hecht, founder, editor
mernaanna@yahoo.com

ISBN: 978-1-63398-068-6

Published by Chatwin Books for the Stories of Arrival project.

For orders and inquiries:

Chatwin Books
Seattle, Washington
www.chatwinbooks.com
info@chatwinbooks.com

WITH GRATEFUL ACKNOWLEDGEMENT
OF GENEROUS SUPPORT FROM:

Institute for Poetic Medicine
Jack Straw Cultural Center
King County 4 Culture
The Satterberg Foundation

TABLE OF CONTENTS

Sahra Hirsi

Dedicated to the voices and visions of our wise young poets.

We who notice Mother Earth's pleas for help, this is for you.

—from the poem "Children of Mother Earth" by Jesfer Lee Agustin

Together, we are strong, together we will raise our voices,
we will stand strong for the only home we have.

—from the poem "Dear Human" by Ramatoulaye Barry

INTRODUCTIONS

Words from Merna Ann Hecht, Project Founder, Co-Director, and Teaching Artist

IT IS MY DEEP HONOR TO EXTEND A WELCOME to the reader of this poetry anthology. At this time in our world, it is paramount to offer young people an opportunity to reflect on how we are caring for the earth and each other. In full recognition that the earth is the only home we have, the students in this year's project have written with compassion and wisdom about steps that could lead us toward creating a far less violent world. They recognize that the earth is the source of the food and water on which we all depend for survival. Their poems remind us of the terrible human and environmental consequences of war and ask us to show respect for the earth and to work toward creating safe, diverse and welcoming communities for all people.

These young people write with the dignity and presence of heart and mind we would hope to find in our world leaders and in our own country's leaders. Instead, the words we long to hear, sadly lacking from far too many governments and politicians, arise from these poets who remind us first hand of the costs of mistreating what sustains us. Caring for the earth and each other, our theme for this year's poetry project, is timelier than we could have anticipated.

My greatest hope is that this year's participants, who wrote so ardently and honestly about their experiences and about protecting the planet, will know that their words matter. I want them to know that their voices can contribute to dispelling the dangerous stereotyping and false words about refugees and immigrants that are far too present in our national and global rhetoric. And, I want them to treasure their profound insights as to the state of the planet and to trust that they can become key spokesmen and women working toward our collective activism for care-taking the earth.

The students in this year's project are some of the strongest and most insightful ambassadors for peace I have encountered anywhere in any situation. One of our Somali students writes about war with uncommon beauty and eloquence using the metaphor of the ocean as a call to peace: *The ocean is calling us / the tides are bringing peace / but we can't hear / because of the war / we changed the water into blood / and the beautiful waves that have always been there / have gone to jail for a long time now.*

That widespread environmental degradation and the unspeakable anguish of war appear in numerous poems in this anthology is no surprise, since many of the students have left their homelands due to inhumane and unlivable conditions. One of our Filipino students speaks with sadness and hope when he writes, *I am a son of the Philippines / Where my ancestors talk with the heart of the land / Before the land was taken by the Spaniards / Before the land was crying with blood / Before my people fought back and claimed the land back / And won the crying land and the rare plants that bloom at night.*

Poetry is a place that allows us to wrap words around our deepest sorrows and our fondest hopes, our praise-songs and our grief songs. Outpourings of loss and joy, memory and courage, shape every poem in this book. Indeed, it is a diverse and varietal garden of expression and emotion and in essence it is a garden of peace. I invite you to stand up for and with these young people providing them with the honor, respect and support they so deserve. They are my teachers and my inspiration and I trust they will be yours too.

—Merna Ann Hecht

Words from Carrie Stradley, Project Co-Director and Foster High School English Language Learning Teacher

INSIDE THIS ANTHOLOGY IS NOT MERELY A UNIT OF POETRY carved out of a school year, but the opportunity to bear witness and honor the lives of these incredible youth. Throughout the project I have witnessed my students grow in their willingness to share of themselves, in their command of the English language, and in their ever-evolving identities of themselves in the landscape of a new country. Not only did they develop the fine art of crafting poetry by deliberating over word choice, but also they have experienced a new way to use their voices with expression rather than the utilitarian English they use to navigate their daily lives. They have deepened their understanding of each other as a community, seeing beyond differences of religion or ethnicity, and finding solidarity as immigrants and refugees. While so much aims to divide us, watching students come together in this project has been equally important as the writing process itself.

A single test can never show the impact this work has had on my students, and its positive effects will last much longer. I'm honored and humbled to work with these remarkable youth, who have shared with us so generously excerpts of their own lives. The project uses poetry to transport culture and transcend time, serving to record the humanity in history in their own words.

—Carrie Stradley

Let us believe we have to take care of the earth,
Let us plant more trees,
Let us grow our food without chemicals, poisons, or toxins,
Let us grow healthy food because the earth is in hunger.
Let us take care of the planet; let us do our job.

—*Anass, Josue, Salina, and Zahid*

CARING FOR THE EARTH AND EACH OTHER: A NEW COLLABORATION

by Merna Ann Hecht

This is the seventh year of the Stories of Arrival Project and thus our seventh poetry anthology. For our last book, in 2015, we partnered with Project Feast (projectfeast.org). Our focus was on creating poetry about the connections we all carry to food and gardens of home countries and cultures. We also addressed food scarcity and hunger and the challenges to adjusting to foods and traditions encountered in a new country far from home. The collaboration resulted in a beautifully illustrated book of poetry and recipes, titled *Our Table of Memories: Food and Poetry of Spirit, Homeland and Tradition*, published by Chatwin Books, available at independent bookstores and on-line.

Our emphasis last year on food and gardens provided a meaningful springboard from which to expand the connections to food into how we should care for the land and by extension how we should care for each other. From this, we developed the idea that we would shape the poetry project around broad issues of "Caring for the Earth and Each Other," because it signified poems that would speak to stewarding the earth and to honoring home countries, loved ones and ourselves.

Discussions about environmental justice, food justice, and our interconnections to the earth and each other took place throughout our project. We were fortunate to welcome different guests to the classroom to deepen these topics. Our intent this year was to support our students in speaking out about Climate Change and Environmental Justice as well as to tell their own "stories of arrival" from areas of intense conflict, and other pressing issues such as poverty, lack of health care, lack of education and environmental degradation. Writing poems about their own experiences of forced migration, life in refugee camps, immigration and about their insights into how we should care for the earth and each other was at the heart of this year's project.

The Namaste Garden Collaboration

We are most fortunate that the International Rescue Committee's (IRC) Namaste Garden is located directly behind Foster High School, literally in the school's back yard, only a five minute walk away! The Namaste Garden is a part of the IRC New Roots Program, which also has a focus on youth programs that support learning about food systems and sustainability from a social justice perspective. The proximity of the garden and the programs designed for young people gave us an ideal collaborative relationship for our project.

The IRC New Roots Programs are located throughout the U. S. in cities that have local IRC branches. These programs provide community garden spaces in which refugees grow their own food much like they did in their home countries. The focus is on food access and the nutritional needs of families upon arrival in the U.S. The program builds on the agricultural experience of many new refugee and immigrant families. The Tukwila IRC New Roots garden serves over 97 refugee families and has nearly 30,000 square feet of land in production.

Many of the students' families have their own plot in the Namaste garden, some proudly garden there themselves and others worked as summer interns through the IRC Youth Food Justice program. Our students were enthusiastic about creating poems in celebration of the Namaste garden and the gardens in their own homelands as well. On a beautiful, sunny autumn day, we walked to the garden, where we were warmly welcomed. We toured the garden plots, the sheds, greenhouses and composting areas. Then we placed our poems around the garden hanging them on branches and fence posts in different garden areas. Next, we were all given various tasks. We leaned into them with the delight of working the land and tending to what the garden needs to grow and flourish.

WELCOMING VISITORS TO THE CLASSROOM

Deepa Iyer visited our classes several times bringing us learning about food systems, food security, and food and environmental justice with her wonderful spirit and many fun improv games that supported new learning on these topics. Deepa is the Field and Education Specialist for the International Rescue Committee's New Roots Program and she leads the Youth Food Justice component. She hails from Oakland, CA where she took a major role in creating a highly successful Youth Food Justice and Intergenerational Gardening Program in partnership with Oakland's International High School with an all refugee and immigrant population. The IRC's Youth Food Justice Program is a cornerstone of New Roots' environmental education efforts. The mission of the program states: "New Roots is about healthy families, secure communities, and a more sustainable future. It's about dignity, determination, and the boundless possibility of human connection. And it's about the power of people to heal and nurture positive change from the ground up."

Through Deepa, we welcomed **Leika Suzumura** and **Shamso Isaak** to work with our classes. They brought their knowledge and expertise of food systems and food and environmental justice to our students with innovative and lively participatory activities. Leika and Shamso are amazing activists in the food and food justice world. Leika is a nutritionist and has done impressive work with Community Kitchens, bringing people together around making food and sharing their cultures. Shamso started the food justice and policy advocacy organization called Living Well Kent, and does powerful work engaging youth in policy change.

Claudia Castro Luna was Seattle's first Civic Poet, and was recently selected to serve as the new WA State Poet Laureate. She is the first immigrant and woman of color to hold this honored position. Claudia presented a two hour poetry workshop to each of our classes. Her experience of coming to the USA at the age of fourteen fleeing the violent Civil War in El Salvador was deeply resonant for the students. Along with her genuine warmth and expertise as a consummate teacher and poet, she brought Walt Whitman's poetry and the words of Chief Sealth and Pope Francis to inspire the students to write about protecting and caretaking the earth. (www.castroluna.com)

Melissa Koch, visual artist, environmentalist, and youth and elder arts mentor, is a widely exhibited artist who has won many awards for her uniquely creative collection. Her work appears in public art installations and in numerous art galleries and exhibitions. Melissa brought her vast knowledge of indigenous culture and art into her upbeat, engaging visual arts workshop with each class. She carried box after box filled with of all manner of art supplies to the classroom. The paints, inks, pens, stickers, stamps and wood and paper palettes from which students could choose resulted in the illustrations which fill the pages of our book. (www.melissakochfinearts.com)

Ohnmar Dandi is the Community Burmese liaison for the Tukwila School District. Her desire to help make a difference for refugees who've gone through so much has led to her current work in the district. Ohnmar speaks Burmese, Karen, Thai and English. Her vision for the Burmese community is to wash away their fear and help them engage with the educational system. She wants each family to understand how powerful family involvement is and she also wants educators to learn about their students' cultural background to better understand their needs.

When Ohnmar visited our classes and presented her powerful poem, she asked the students to close their eyes and hold hands, thus connecting the entire class by hands and hearts as they listened and visualized the losses that war brings. A somber, deeply respectful silence filled the classroom as Ohnmar's vivid metaphors representing landmines, bullets and the destructive effects of war on the environment affected each of us. We were honored that Ohnmar shared her profoundly sensitive and impactful poem of love and loss with each class.

WALK WITH ME (YOU WILL SEE WHAT I SEE)

by Ohnmar Dandi

This poem is dedicated to the students who escape from Burma. I want the educator and the students to feel what they feel, beyond their own lives, so they can support their education with understanding of the Burmese students' background and experience.

Walk with me, Walk with me
Hold my hand tight
Please, hold my hand tight and walk with me
You will see what I see; you will see what I see.

Walk with me, Walk with me
There is a beautiful star, a sparkling star, smiling at me.
The star that I saw was not in the sky, flying above me.
That star had a song and fire, as when the bullets touch each other.
As a child, I knew that I should be hiding deep underground.

That is the star, the star that is in my land.
Do you see what I see? Do you see what I see?

Walk with me. Hold my hand, you will see what I see;
you will see what I see.

Walk with me, Walk with me
There is a flower, a beautiful yellow flower sharp in my eyes.
I love it, I want to pick up the flower and let it stay near me.
I run to pick up the flower from the field like a princess flying in the garden,
My grandfather grabs me like a ball before it falls to the ground,
He tells me that is a land mine under all the flowers
that can cut my body into small pieces.
That flower was an illusion, we all stood on the ground of land mines.

That is the flower, the flower that is my land
Do you see what I see? Do you see what I see?
Walk with me. Hold my hand, you will see what I see;
you will see what I see.

Walk with me, Walk with me
There is a river, neutral green water near the bush,
I am thirsty and I had a long day's walk under the sun,
over the mountain and across the desert.
I will refresh myself, clean myself
and energize my mind to have a better mood.
My best friend's fighter dog jumped into the river barking at me
I thought he was funny, the fighter dog angered me that day,
not letting me drink the water.
That water has poison in it.
Poisoned waters that can harm my whole body.

That is the water, the water that is in my land.
Do you see what I see? Do you see what I see?
Walk with me. Hold my hand, you will see what I see;
you will see what I see.

Walk with me, Walk with me
You are about to let go of my hand,
I had to let it go from my brother when I saw the star,
I lost my grandpa when I saw the flower,
I had to free my dog when I found the water.

Are you still holding my hand?
I fear you will not see what I see,
Please still hold my hand tight
and don't let it go.
Do you see what I see?
Do you see what I see?

We Speak For Ourselves and Our Countries

artwork: Josue Tebalan

WELCOME TO VIETNAM

Nhan Nguyen

Vietnam is part of my heart
the busy sounds of cars and bicycles
running like a tiger almost catching his food
the smoke of cars killing the plants.

Ring the bell for no reason,
old people wake up early,
drink black coffee and exercise with friends
at the green park,
but in my mind they are in the big green forest
they want to go back to childhood,
have fun with friends
and become good friends again,
like a thunderbolt, they want to go back in time.

Don't worry, when you go to Vietnam
you will make friends easily
the flowers are growing on the street
but the stained air is making the flowers become old
near dying, as if at peace, as in death.
I almost feel like I've lost something
because of the smell of the dead flowers
I know the flowers are crying.

But Vietnam stays deep in my heart,
if I lost my country, I would feel
like I lost my heart,
my legs are set on Vietnam
and never leave.

I love the heat of my country
that makes my skin change to brown,
I love my brown skin.
What Vietnam has is in my body.
I know my Vietnamese people sometimes show bad
thinking
but I always love my country,
all my respect I give to Vietnam,
like I do to my parents.

I always remember what my grandparents said
"COME BACK."
My promise never changes
believe me, Vietnam,
I will see you soon
I love you, my country.

I Am a Son of Tarlac

Gavin Dylan Garcia

I am a son of Tarlac
Where my family lives in a fresh green rural place in Camiling
Where I wear my off-white uniform with black shoes
Where I inhale the scent of green leaves.

I am the son of Tarlac
Where my ancestors worked hard for the new generation
Where people strive for their family's bright future.

I am the son of Tarlac
Where the poor farmers and their "Hacienda" lands were taken
And the fresh grass was burnt down by Japanese and Spanish people
Where Corazon Aquino, our former president, fought for the farmers' rights.

I am the son of Tarlac
Where the biggest drug laboratory in the Philippines is located,
Where gunshots are heard by our scared ears,
Where people discriminate you for being ugly, poor, or just low quality.

I am the son of Tarlac
A small, wise and smart city,

Slowly but surely improving its economy,
But the ancestors' lands are being demolished
By workers who have no hearts,
The wonders of the Philippines like Bohol, Palawan, and Baguio
Are crowded, becoming ruined by brainless people
Who try to make a change.

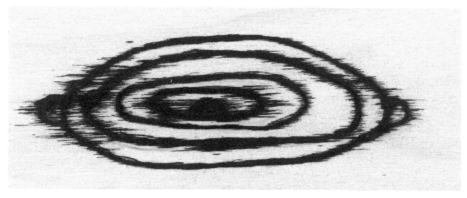

Naing Thang

MY MEMORIES

Mhilz Ang

The colorful memories of my childhood
are memories of when I wandered out of the spooky blue woods,
and memories of when the black spiders crawled on my back.

I remember the green tree house where I jumped with my friends
when I chased my friend to the tree
and when I climbed up the green tallest tree.

I remember when my mom taught me how to be me
the time she said, "Be what you want to be,"
the time I said to myself, "When I grow up I will be successful because of me."

I remember my island out of thousands of beautiful islands, why was I in Cebu,
my challenging island Cebu, was I really meant to live there?
Will my dark life be successful when I'm in back in Cebu?

I remember the times I crawled and cried from my broken shell
when I almost broke all of my shell,
the times I shouted to myself,
"Remember what your mother said,
be what you want to be!"

I will always remember the time my father whipped me with his iron belt
and the time when all boastful people hated me
and the time I starved myself and cried all night.

I remember the times that they compared me to people
I couldn't compete with for my grades,
the times when they said you're the only one
in the family that has low grades,
the time when I promised myself,
one day you all will be kneeling in front of me
because of what I achieved.

I remember how I got through all those problems
without anyone but myself,
the time I said thanks to all of you,
this wouldn't happen without those problems you gave to me,
the time that I said to myself,
"You did it! You have achieved your dream!"

MEMORIES OF LOST ONES

Chi Hlaing Tun

Why, why can't I remember the small green pond by my house in Thailand
that miraculous water flowing down the mountain to the small pond.
Why can't I remember how beautiful the cross was, and how much love
my villagers had for the Lord.

Why can't I forget my mom's strong papaya tree being defeated by the mighty lightning,
getting struck by the lightning, and falling on my hay house,
and at that moment I wondered,
was the papaya tree, I thought so strong, really that strong?

Why can't I forget the destructive war killing thousands of my people,
the red burning light with moving spikes,
the black cloud that could kill you if you just took a breath.
Why can't I remember the color of the red rising sun,
rising from the blue lake to the red sky
to show the white land. My Karen* flag doesn't wave for nothing,
its color can be the water that takes out the burning red light of war,
that color can also be a gas mask, that can help us breathe through the black cloud.

*Karen (pronounced Kah-REN) people are indigenous to the Thailand-Burma border region in Southeast Asia and are one of the many ethnic groups in Burma. They have fled their homeland to escape killings, torture, rape, landmines and forced labor by the Burmese military regime. Thousands of Karen refugees cross the border to Thailand for safety and live in one of twelve refugee camps. The refugee camps appear as extremely large villages of bamboo and thatch buildings along the Thai-Burma border. Hundreds of thousands of people live in these camps; many are eventually resettled to third countries. (source: https://ethnomed.org/culture/karen/karen-cultural-profile)

Who I Am

Chi Hlaing

I'm a child of God, created in His image.
My actions should reflect in God, but I'm only human, and that's all I'll be.
But I can try to show that He's running my life.
I want my actions to reflect Him, like how a mirror reflects me.
He is the one who makes me, me. Without Him I wouldn't be myself.

I am a child of Thailand, Burma, America, and Karen.
My culture is mixed, but like the flour in the water to make dough
I was planted in Thailand, in the land of Bangkok, but blossoming in a refugee camp,
not knowing that the water that nourishes a cherry blossom
is the red flowing blood of my Karen people.

Until this day I don't remember my culture
that's why I get wrapped up in American culture.
I'm disappointed in myself, but at least I still haven't forgotten myself.
I am Chi Hlaing Tun, the son of multiple cultures,
a brother of different religions.

AM I STILL WHO I AM?

Ling Hung Young

Am I still who I am
from a village called Chang
a daughter of my village
who grew up beautifully with her village taking care of her,
my village is my mother and father who I love.
The farm that grew there is in the heart of my village
and it will never be mine again, gone forever.
The tears of my village are like a waterfall I want to stop,
but I let those sad tears float freely.
I came from a needy village to a wealthy country,
yet the heart of my village who raised me like a mother
is still in my soul.
People will change like a season,
yet the mothering spirit of my village is a part of me,
but the moment I fail to remember my village
is the day I lose my memories,
will they be gone forever?
As stars join in the sky every night,
will new memories come into my heart?
Am I still who I am?

My Oppressed Rohingya Peoples

Rujina Bibi Mojullah

I cannot forget how the Myanmar government didn't take care of my people,
how they took away their houses and killed them,
and raped the beautiful girls that they liked.

I cannot forget how human rights are marginalized in Myanmar
where my people are not treated as human beings,
and Aung Sang Suu Kyi is not helping my Rohingya people,
she is staying silent.

I cannot forget that Aung Sang Suu Kyi is supporting the Myanmar government,
that the Myanmar government calls my Rohingya people terrorists
even though they are the first people in Myanmar.

I cannot forget how my Rohingya people are suffering
by not having enough food to eat and a safe place to sleep.

*The Rohingya are an ethnic group, the majority of whom are Muslim, who have lived for centuries in the majority Buddhist Myanmar, or Burma as many still call it. They are not considered one of the country's 135 official ethnic groups and have been denied citizenship in Myanmar since 1982, which has effectively rendered them stateless. Nearly all of the Rohingya in Myanmar live in the western coastal state of Rakhine and are not allowed to leave without government permission. It is one the poorest states in the country with ghetto-like camps and a lack of basic services and opportunities. Due to ongoing violence and persecution, hundreds of thousands of Rohingya have fled to neighboring countries either by land or boat over the course of many decades. At this time the violence against them is at a critical point as thousands pour into Bangladesh to save their lives. (https://tinyurl.com/rohingya-SOAP)

WHO AM I

Naing Thang

I am a male,
Born to be boy.
I am a son.
I am a big brother in my family.
I am someone who cares about my friends.
I am Asia.
I am Burma.
I am a teen who has a big family, six people in my home.
I am from running away because of Burma's many civil wars.
I am from a refugee family.
I am a product of war and displacement.
I am now in America.
I'm a translator sitting down in a chair.
I am a helper, helping refugees like me.
I help them go to school.
I teach them English.
I am Asia, I am Burma, I am America.

Pabi Gajmer

I Have the Right to Speak

Monica Hniang Dawt Chin

I speak for my country, Myanmar not to have war.
I speak for my community, Hakha, to become family.
I speak for my school to have access to education.
I speak for my people to have their freedom and rights.
I speak for the soldiers that fight for our country.
I speak for the injustice in our world.
I speak for the civil rights of immigrants.
I speak for my country to have freedom.
I speak for my house to shine bright.
I speak for my religion to have freedom from discrimination.
I speak for Burma's land reform.
I speak for Burma, my country, to have clean water.
I speak for my country to have enough nourishing food.
I speak for those who grow plants to have enough water.
I speak for my grandmother to live longer.

Memories

Ling Hung Young

I remember the name of the flowers
that made my country Burma look beautiful
giving me good memories of how I grew up
and keeping my memories for me.

I remember the farm that kept me safe,
and the birds that woke me up every morning,
but I cannot remember the trees
waving at me each morning,
I am ashamed to forget those trees
who gave me fresh air in the hot summer
when there was no fan.

I cannot forget the bumpy roads that burned and hurt
my people's legs, the red, sharp rocks that seemed hungry
to eat at our legs, we who wore no slippers, no boots, only bare feet,
I cannot forget those struggles.

I cannot forget the market that takes a thousand miles
from my village to get there,
and I cannot forget the violence that bothers my beautiful land,
that bothers all of my people,
why can't I just let it go, why can't I forget?

MY COUNTRY BURMA

Naing Thang

My country, Burma, please stop wars,
make the country peaceful.

BANG!

Guns used in wars.
Run or die,
loved ones fall with them or die.

Only if we stop war then the country will know peace,
stop workers from fighting each other.

Burma is filled with many wars,
cities and villages fighting each other.

I wish I could change the past,
forget the past and start a new life.
Burma thank you for making history,
thank you Burma, for starting a new history
with a generation that lives in peace.

When I Think of My Country

Naing Thang

When I think of Burma
how people start saying bad things about it
I think of visiting my country again.

      Bright as a flashlight.

I hear the sounds of elephants,
I can see my people changing
as if they are the next generation,
people are loving,
the birds are dancing like humans,
my memories fight with me,
and I know at that moment I love
my country and my people.

MOVING TOWARD

Chandra Biswa

Just got home from a friend's house,
"We are going to America."
My body froze like snow on the great Himalayan mountains,
heard the news from my parents,
questions pop up inside my head,
"Why are we going to America," I shout!
Dad answers, "We need a better living place,
I want you to have a better education."
Got my home phone and called my friends Anisha and Dolma
"Hey we are going to America! Huh," I said.
We cried on the phone,
"I will miss you."
My heart boiled over with deep sadness.
What am I going to do without all of my friends?
That night my tears covered me instead of my blanket.
Three days left, the house was all empty,
just an hour left before our flight,
all the neighbors came to my house
our tears fell down as we embraced
one last time,
"I am going to miss all of you,"
I said, as we gathered our lives in several bags
and boarded the International Organization for Migration bus
full of others headed from Nepal to America.
Waving my hand with sorrow and also with curiosity,
I wonder if I will ever see my friends again.

NEPALI KITCHEN

Pratichya Biswa

The sound and the smell have been with me since birth
but when the earthquake destroyed all my peoples' kitchens
I missed those sounds and those smells,
the sizzling oil and the tinging sound of stirring of *maasu*.

The kitchen that brought my family all together disappeared,
all of our hearts were broken,
we lost our family members-brothers, sisters,
some of us lost our parents.

All these things happened in front of my eyes
watching from afar, and I was helpless.
I felt paralyzed, just sitting there and watching
all that was destroyed by the earthquake.

Sometimes people wish for so many things,
but they can't always have what they wish for
or what they want.
Just like that, I wish for my peoples' kitchens
and their houses to be safe.
But, will my wish come true or only halfway true,
even with my fingers crossed and my heart beating fast
not all of my peoples' kitchens and houses were safe.

I Speak for Myself

Salina Biswa

I am a refugee
my parents are from Bhutan
the stories of their country live inside of me,
myself, a daughter of Nepal,
a land with dirty water
where children play in water pools
created from hard rain.

I am from the land of Nepal,
rice fields flow from the earth like green steps,
the orange seed of the rice grain
blooms into the world.

I am proud of my family,
my mom and dad,
my brother Sagar and my sister Sajita,
my family who supports me and my dreams.

As a daughter of Nepal
I will always remember my hometown,
Beldangi Two Refugee Camp,
and as a child how I played hopscotch
and marbles in the busy streets.

Rujina Bibi Mojullah

THE EARTHQUAKE IN NEPAL

Krinsuk Rai

We were sitting down
talking about school and how the day went,
the ground started shaking
but my heart was beating, moving faster,
I was worried like an ant being stepped on,
it was for nearly 20 seconds
but felt like hours.
Then my mom said, "come here,"
we hid under a table
as if someone was looking for us,
people were screaming in other houses
as if they saw a ghost.
Then, it stopped moving, it was silent.

The Day I Left Nepal

Krinsuk Rai

I remember the beautiful place next to my house
something I would see every day
when I woke up,
it was the river, flowing downhill,
sunflowers along the bank,
it was like a mother guarding her children.

I will never forget the day when I left all of my friends,
and all the goodbyes I said,
thy day when I left my country and came to America
as a refugee from Nepal.
And I will never forget my mother's stories
of leaving everything behind in Bhutan
and how she had to run away.

MEMORIES OF MY CULTURAL FESTIVE DRESS

Salina Biswa

I remember the dress of my culture
Gurung, dark red and bright yellow stripes,
we can wear our cultural dress at Dashain,
Indra Jatra, Constitution Day, Samvidhaan Diwas,
Culture Day, but on a regular day for me
I can only wear normal home clothes.

But on holidays, when I go to my cousin's home
on our cultural celebrations,
whenever other people see my dress
they say, "Oh that dress looks so beautiful and amazing
with hot pink and dark sky blue and white designs,"
I act like I don't hear the words
because when people from other countries visit my country
they like to wear our cultural clothes, but they do not understand
our culture's dress, even now American people
also wear our dresses, even if they are beautiful or colorful
when they wear our cultural dress, they don't understand
or respect our culture, our festivals, or our ancestors.

I remember when I went shopping for Dashain
I asked to the man to show me *lehenga*,*

but he showed me the *choli*,*
the color was light grey and soft pink,
it did not even look good on me,
when I told him I needed a different design
he yelled at me, saying, "I don't have *lehenga*,"
so I had to buy *choli*.

Now I wish I could go back to Nepal
I wish I could go to the beautiful Bangay market again.

*Nepali traditional dress is a long skirt worn as a bottom portion, with a choli (blouse). Lehenga are long skirts worn on festivals and special events, while Ghagra or Chaniya are traditional skirts worn on a day to day basis by girls and women. (https://www.quora.com/What-is-the-difference-between-lehenga-ghagra-and-chaniya)

The Bangay Market is a small market near the Beldangi and Pathri refugee camps in Nepal. As of April 2014, the International Organization for Migration (IOM) that is responsible for the refugees' resettlement has said that 89,000 refugees have been resettled in eight different countries. (Wikipedia: Beldangi Refugee Camps)

I SPEAK TO THE FUTURE

Andrew Rai

Son, I want you to know how we came to America.

Daughter, I want you to know how to cook our culture's food
like *roti*, *wacheepa* and *safala*.

Son, I want you to understand that you have to know our Nepali language.

Daughter, I want you to understand that you have to know our culture like *Dasai*.

Son, please remember that you are from Nepal, and you are a son of Nepal.

Daughter, please remember that you are from Nepal
and you have to know that we have one God,
yet know that we have many religions there.

Son, I want you to know the word *Namasta* in our language
because it means to give respect and it is part of our culture.

Daughter, I want you to know the word *Jaimasee* in our language
because it means you have to show your respect to others
and this is important because if you respect them they will respect you.

Chandra Biswa

I Speak for Myself

Zahid Ortiz

I am he who wonders why the U.S. deports people
he who questions why is he here
he who hopes to see his family again
he who dreams to be better everyday
he who wishes to graduate.

I speak for my country
my country in Central America
my small but united country
my beautiful country.
My country with its blue and white flag,
the blue color represents the ocean
the white color represents the peace.

I speak for my country where we used to go to the river
and we would climb trees and swing high above the river
let go, spin around, and jump into the water,
where once we used our sling shots,
caught iguanas, brought them home, cooked them,
and ate them, until we were caught!

I speak for myself, he who is proud
of his country's hardworking people,

cutting cane with machetes, planting corn in large fields,
taking care of each other with a government that doesn't care
about peoples' rights, or their safety, or bringing justice
to those who need to be punished.

He who is proud of his country because though a small country,
it is a country of courage.

Sahra Hirsi

TO MY FUTURE CHILDREN, FOR HONDURAS

Carmen J. Hernandez

Son, I want you to know, *que yo soy parte de otro país también,*
that I am part of another country too.

Daughter, I want you to know, *que ustedes tienen también parte de la sangre honduras,*
that you also have part of the blood of Honduras.

Son, I want you to understand, *es muy importante que ustedes sepan,*
it is very important that you know.

Daughter, I want you to understand, *que somos parte de Honduras,*
that we are part of Honduras.

Son, please remember, *que eres parte de Honduras,*
that you are part of Honduras.

Daughter, please remember that you are, *responsable de recorda de donde eres,*
responsible for remembering where you are from.

Son, know that you came from a place, *donde hay muchas personas amigables,*
personas trabajadoras, y paisajes hermosos con montañas,
where there are many friendly people, hardworking people,
and beautiful landscapes with mountains.

Daughter, know that you came from a place, *donde hay muchos rios, playas, animales,*
where there are many rivers, beaches, and animals.

Naming Myself

Zahid Ortiz

He who was born in Honduras,
He who misses his beautiful country in Central America,
He who misses the flora and fauna, the *guacamaya*,
the *venado*, the *cola blanca*, the *orquidia* petals
like white stars on long green branches.

He whose skin is the color of brown pride,
He who misses his country
because the morning is filled with soft clouds in wide skies
with morning stars, where that sky and the ocean
are interchangeable.

He who wants everyone to know
that Honduras is more than gangs,
that Honduras is more than perfect beaches.
He who wants everyone to know
that Hondurans were the first to care for, raise and harvest
the strong beans that are made into coffee
that is poured into coffee cups all over the world.

THE STORY OF MY STRANGE TEARS

Wasim Azizi

I remember my best friend Amir
who always showed me the good way
in life, like a teacher.

I remember my first home in Kabul
the mornings with loud horns on the broken street,
the voices of people in the grocery store below my house.

I remember the stories of the feelings of my family
when my grandpa died and the strange tears
of my grandma.

I cannot forget the sound of gun shots,
the voice of an innocent father, saying,
"Someone find my son, he is lost,"
and the bloody tears of the son saying, "Dad, where are you?"

I cannot ever forget the sound of politics,
the broken promises,
the streets, the homes that are not safe,
the families who lost their families,
lost their sons, their children or their parents.

MY LIFE IN MOROCCO

Anass Harma Alaoui

I remember
basstilla that we made with fragile paper,
a thin dough wrapped around fresh chicken or fish
served on a bright blue and white plate
covered and intricate,
larger than a young man's head,
ready for everyone
to eat with their clean right hand.
I remember all the beautiful moroccan food,
basstilla, briwa, makhmar,
and I remember the beautiful fruit of my country
like *fraize, toot, kiwi.*

 MOROCCO.IS.LIFE

Anass Harma Alaoui

SOMALIA, AN OCEAN

Shafi Mohamed Osman

Somalia is an ocean.
Undisturbed it is beautiful,
clear, blue, peaceful.
Disturbed and disrupted,
it is dark, bloody, dangerous.

The ocean is calling us,
the tides are bringing peace,
but we can't hear
because of the war
we changed the water into blood,
and the beautiful waves that have always been there
have gone to jail for a long time now.

The ocean is crying
because we let her down,
we smashed her to the ground
and denied her any chance for peace
as if we don't need the ocean
but we long for her
to see the reflection of our beauty in her.

Somalia, it is time to open our eyes
and see how the ocean looks today.

Somalia, it is time to free the ocean,
it is time for the ocean to rise
like the flag that stands for peace.

Let the ocean tides bring us peace.
Somalia, it is time to welcome
the ocean and open our hearts.

Let us come together
be undisturbed in peace,
let us come together
and let the water be clear once more,
and we shall not let our blood touch the water again.

artwork: Najmo M. Abdi

Let us Free The ocean
like The birds, let The ocean
swimm in Peace, it is time
to welcome The ocean

Shafi Mohamed Osman

As the Green Plants Need Water

Shafi Mohamed Osman

When I think of my country
I think of struggle,
it is bright as the sun
and I can hear its beautiful voice.
Yet, I can see it needs help
as the green plants need water,
Somalia, I am coming for you.

Inhumanity

Sahra Hirsi

The sound of war in my country, Somalia
Covering your ears from the explosions
Running soldiers
Hiding away from the guns
Children playing with the guns
Innocent people getting killed
Birds falling down.

SOMALI FLAG

Shafi Mohamed Osman

I remember the soft blue of the Indian ocean
with white capped waves
and the sky with the proud blue flag of Somalia.

I remember that to respect our people
we have to let them live their own lives,
and the responsibility we have is to let our country be
a peaceful place,
and our Somali flag is what my people deserve
when they look at the single star in the middle.

I remember the peaceful respect for the flag
that still stands tall,
the flag when it waves
that brings happiness
to the smallest and largest,
and the flag that can unite us
and make us strong enough.

And I cannot forget
blood that flows
to the ground
without reason
and the bodies
that will not see
their home again,
or the war that killed thousands
of young, elderly and middle aged men,
women, and children, their innocent lives gone.

Why do some believe
the war is better
than peace?
Why? Why? Why?

A GIRL WITH A DREAM

Sahra Hirsi

I'm someone who loves singing,
I'm someone who loves to help others,
I'm someone who worries about other people who have nothing.
I'm a girl from the Hirsi family,
I'm a student in Foster High School,
I'm a daughter with fourteen siblings,
I'm someone who has dreams.
Dreams of going to university studying how to be a lawyer.
Dreams of buying my mother a house in Dubai.
Dreams of building houses in Somalia
for the ones that have no place to live in.
Dreams of succeeding in life.

Identifying Myself

Samsam Hirsi

I am a daughter of the Hirsi family,
I am a sister of fifteen siblings,
I am a student,
I am someone who offers a smile to everyone.
I am a girl who wears every color
of Hijab—pink, black, maroon,
whose eyes are dark,
whose skin is the color of almonds.
I am a hardworking person,
I am a proud Muslim,
I am from Somalia,
I am full Somali,
I am someone who cares about your pain,
emotion and culture.
I am a person who wishes
to graduate from university,
to study law and become a lawyer.
I am a hopeful person,
I am a helpful person,
I am a person who wants to have a successful life.
I am a person who tries everything that's new to me.
I am organized.
I am a person who talks about great decisions.
I am person who believes in herself,
I am your other half.

I SPEAK FOR MYSELF

Najmo Abdi

I speak for my country Kenya
I speak for my village
I speak for my family
I speak for my friends
I speak for the people who don't have a voice
I speak for my people
I speak for Justice to be served
I speak for my mom, dad, brother, and sister
I speak for police brutality against citizens
I speak for women's rights
I speak for #blacklivesmatter
I speak for immigrant rights
I speak for civil rights
I speak for access to education
I speak for the Dakota Pipeline
I speak for poverty
I speak for the low income families
I speak for discrimination based on sexual orientation
I speak for the elderly abused in nursing homes
I speak for mental health problems and addiction
I speak for freedom of speech that is prohibited in some countries
I speak for freedom of all religions.

Ahku Kuedituka

My Rancho

Josue Tebalan

If my *rancho* could speak
it would tell me to pick up my garbage,
plastic bottles, fast food,
and animals who lost their lives to drunk drivers.

If my *rancho* could speak
it would warn me
not to let bad people in,
drunk neighbors, gang members, and *narcos*.

If my *rancho* could speak
it would tell of the generations of farmers
who have built the *rancho*
Mi abuela Senaida y mi abuelo.

If my *rancho* could sing
it would sing songs of all
the beautiful places in *el rancho*,
like the field, *malecon, y las playas*
full of people on Saturdays and Sundays.

If my *rancho* could warn me,
it would warn me not to do drugs
it would warn me to stay in school
it would warn me to respect all life in the *rancho*.

Memories of Nairobi

Mohamed Mogow

When I think of Nairobi I remember the beautiful Acacia trees,
branches spread out to the skies,
the proud, smiling faces of hard working men,
the smiling faces of children playing soccer,
the steep, powerful waterfalls deep in the jungles
and the last time my grandfather kissed me
on the forehead when I came to visit.

I remember my grandmother's excited face
when she saw me walking up to her door,
and I remember the dirty soccer ball I used to play with
in the sandy ground of Nairobi.

And I will never forget the ferocious face of the warthog
who killed my friend in Nairobi,
or the bullies I used to fight in Nairobi
because of their disrespect to me.
And I will never forget my little brother who died in childbirth,
and my big sister who died of natural causes.

And I will not forget the pollution all over
the neighborhood every morning,
or the struggling faces of starving people in Nairobi,
or the many people who died of natural causes,
or the many other people who were killed every day in Nairobi.

IN MY HOME SCHOOL

Ramatoulaye Barry

I remember the out loud laughing of the students
in my elementary school in Conakry,
running everywhere in the compound of the school,
the beautiful voices of the girls who sang and jumped rope
in the corridors of the school during lunch.

I remember how the students' arms proudly lifted up in all classes,
clapping their fingers, and shouting in a melodious voice,
"Moi Monsieur, Moi Monsieur," to attract the teacher's attention,
and the happy and confused face of the teacher
wondering who he's going to choose.

And I remember the cry of my friends,
and the violent voice of the black whip
every time the teacher beat one of them,
starting with the first in line, beaten sometimes for:
the wrong uniform
the wrong answer
the wrong grades
being tardy
having no homework or notebook
disturbing the class.
Beaten for these that we couldn't avoid at school.

I remember how my legs were trembling
and sweating simultaneously because I was the next,
I remember the fast beating and strong rhythm of my heart
like the vibration of a nightclub,
the angry face of the teacher,
and the innocent face of mine.

But in my home school,
I have gained a second kind and rare family,
from them I learned what love is
and how to live in solidarity,
what peace is, and how to have patience.

We all have a start place and an end place,
my home school is my start place.

I KNOW WHO I AM

Epha Ngoy

I'm Epha, a daughter of God,
a girl of peace,
a princess of the universe,
the one and only Joelle Muamine's daughter.

I'm someone who loves music
and who loves to have a good relationship
with different people and races.

I'm the tree planted near the river
I'm in a generation of Abraham.

I am what I am,
I am the angel of my body,
I'm African, a young dreamer,
I am one of many heroines
in Africa and in America.
I'm a singer,
I'm a student from Foster High School,
I'm funny, but I get mad easily
when I don't appreciate something
that someone says or does.

I'm Epha Ngoy, Princess Florianna, Beyoncé in Christ,
La fille en couleur, aka smart girl.

THE MUSIC IS MY LIFE

Epha Ngoy

I began to sing
when I was five years old.
The first song that I sang
in my life in front of more than a hundred people
was the song YESU, NA LINGI YO
which means, Jesus, I Love You.

I still remember my primary school in Congo
Complexe Scolaire Elu when we sang
every Friday before going home.
And I remember all that I sacrificed for the music,
my sleep, my time, my holidays,
and even when I was sick I woke up and sang.

But when I told my Mom
that I had to stop singing,
because I didn't have much time
to take care of myself,
she looked at me with tears in her eyes
and answered me,
The music is your life!

ETHIO

Tewodros Sisay

I remember my country Ethiopia
its natural places
that look like palaces
with jagged peaks
and historical places
Lalibela, Axum, Fasil castle
which bring tourists every day.

I remember my hospitable country
and her generous people
and her culture
even in an age of mass tourism,
many tourists are still considered
as honored guests,
and we offer hospitality to total strangers.

I remember the Indigenous life,
small rivers, many animals
like Red Fox, *Chlada babool, Waliya,*
found only in my country, Ethiopia.

And I remember the broken roads like crackers
in my city with zig zagged lines of cars
without traffic lights,

with frequent car accidents
at night on dark streets.

I will always remember my childhood friends
and my neighborhood school,
we spent our time together
playing basketball, studying for tests,
fighting in the back of the school.

I have hope for my country,
I hope for development
because she's backwards
to the rest of the world,
I hope for a fair and just government,
a democracy, for all of my people,
I have hope for Ethio.

WHO AM I

Ubah Osman

I am from Ethiopia, but a daughter of Somalia
where my mother and father were born
where they cannot return because of the war.

I am from rations given by the government,
from not enough food, soap, or oil for my family of nine
in the refugee camp.

I am from a garden of vegetables
from hard work and a field of corn,
and from my own hands that love to cook,
I am from rice, coffee and tea
and from days when it was hard to find food.

I am from loving my family
and starting a new life.

Pratichya Biswa

MY BEAUTIFUL COUNTRY BALE ROBE IN ETHIOPIA

Zulalureman Ebro

I remember the day I left my country, Bale Robe in Ethiopia.
I remember Bale Robe of animals, like monkey, *nyala*, and wolf.
I remember my friends who are still in Ethiopia.

And I can't really forget in my life
how I used to help my elders
how they gave me advice such as,
"Go to school, don't get mad about your life,
always to try achieve your goals, don't worry no matter how hard it is.
Likewise, my elders told me, everything will pass,
yoo rabbi jedhe, if Allah says, one day
I will see my beautiful country and my people
so it will come to be."

It touches me when I remember my country,
I remember the sound of my people's voices raised in protests.
I remember my love for my cousin's farm,
picking fruit from the trees.
I remember my two sisters who are still in Ethiopia,
they won't come to the USA
because they have children and they will not leave their children.

Oromia Shall Be Free

Zulalureman Ebro

When I think of the Ethiopian government
I can see generations of people dying and homeless,
Oromia colonized by Ethiopia,
Oromia is our country, but not anymore,
bountiful farms, wealthy establishments, places of learning
were taken by the hands of the Ethiopian government.
To protest meant being killed, beaten, or put in prison.

Ethiopian government degrades Oromo people,
they are racist
they treated Tigray people with justice,
but Oromo people are treated like slaves.
My people escaped the country
to lands around the world,
while others sang of freedom.
Umar Suleyman sang for freedom,
Dubbachunis ca, alisunis dubbin nama dhiba
"It's hard to speak and it's hard to be quiet,"
he protested for years,
so Ethiopia's government tried to silence him,
so he escaped to Norway,
but he is still demanding our rights.

Oromo people do not want
to protest anymore

because they know what will happen if they try to protest,
but that's not true.
Let's stand strong together, that's how we will get our rights.
Inshallah, I hope one day
Oromo people will have their rights.

Zulalureman Ebro

I Speak For Myself

Awet Berhane

I am from the village
three days by car from Asmara.
There are not many people anymore,
most people move to the city
to work in buildings
instead of farms.

When I was a child,
there were animals.
I took care of goats, camels, cows, and chickens,
but now I am in Tukwila, Washington,
a person who takes care of himself,
only myself.
My parents know I am in the U.S.
and I am alone.
If I was home, I would be forced
to be a soldier.
I hope one day my family will come to the U.S.
that is my dream,
and my plan,
to live with them again, forever.

But for now, I speak for myself.

MY COUNTRY

Awet Berhane

Where my people work hard.
Where we eat together the spongy and soft injera.
Where there is dry land and the water shortage.
Where the government killed people in front of me.
Where I will never forget about my friends dying in the jail.
And how can I forget that we are working
for the government for free, hard work, no money.
How can I forget that we don't have our freedom.

I Am Who I Am

Sibhat Gebrekidan

I am alive.
Not just to live, but alive,
I love when my body is moving, dancing,
I love when I taste the beautiful and clean air,
I love when I touch my heart by praising God,
I am alive waking up every morning as if I am the sunrise.

I am Sibhat son of Shewit
I am black, he who came from Eritrea, East Africa,
I am he who comes from the wild
and from the village called Adi Qala.

I am he who came from the refugee camp May Ayni.
I am he who left his country when he was young,
I am he who lived by himself when he was young,
I am the one who has all the responsibility for himself.

I am he who loves classical music and all other music,
I am he who is a hard worker and goes to church on Sunday,
I am he who attends school and works full time,
I am he who loves soccer.

I am he who lives in hope,
I am Sibhat who wants to have a successful life.

BLACK SLAVE: FOR LIBYA*

Sibhat Gebrekidan

I am an African Black slave
I can no longer say I understand this world,
tell me who I am,
tell me where I come from,
just tell me, tell me where I am from,
I have long enough been a slave.

Tell your world in the news, in magazines
we have started to enslave each other,
we have killed our sisters & brothers.

I am hurt, I am broken,
I am screaming loudly,
I am calling to the world,
but there is no one who can save me,
there is no one who can stand by my side
because they don't want to,
they don't want to see my pain.

How can I cry when there are no tears left,
I have been crying long enough,
but they are still doing what they've done before,
enslaving our black brothers and sisters.

I am lonely, there is no family anymore,
I am lonely, they have killed friends.
Where is the humanity in us?
Where is the humanity in being?
Let me ask again,
where is humanity in being?
Because I am still a slave
they sold me like an animal,
who will tell them,
I am a slave,
I am still a slave.

*Just as we were in the final deadline for printing this book, Sibhat heard the news of a breaking story, (November 29, 2017) about the slave trade in Libya and its horrific human rights abuses affecting refugees and migrant workers on whom the world seems to have turned its back. He wrote this poem the same day, to express his sorrow and outrage about this inhumane situation. He hopes it might inspire those who read it to follow up with learning about the situation and learning what they might do to help change it.

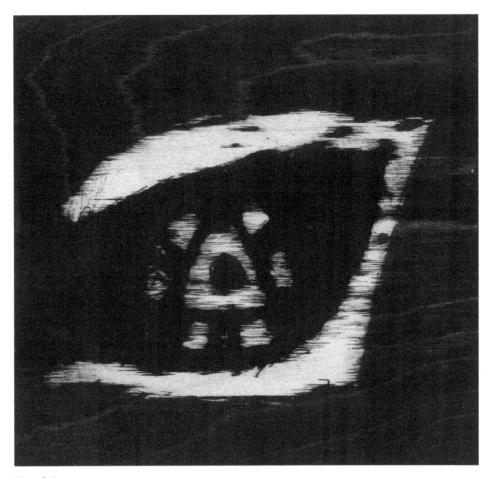

Krinsuk Rai

Roots & Branches:
Poems in Honor of Our Loved Ones

artwork: Monica Hniang Dawt Chin

Sibhat Gebrekidan

THE OLD TREE

Jesfer Lee Agustin

Do not dare underestimate the strength of an old tree
whose root is deeply in the earth,
for like a family who supports each other
through trial and storm,
the old tree root has grown big,
and the tree is deep with his roots.

Since the roots of a tree are like a family,
then you should know a tree that has deep roots
will be sturdy even through a storm.

MI FAMILIA

Gavin Dylan Garcia

The blood that flows in my veins
the passion we share like cooking delicious food
like *Bulalo, Sinigang,* and *Pinakbe*
all grew up in my family.

Sweat dripping and tears shed
all this for an astonishing future was worth it,
a future where we are wealthy enough to live a healthy life.

Now we know new generations must continue living
from the roots of our ancestors
to the successful leaves of our family tree.

"Lupang Hinirang" is our national anthem
about heroes who fought for our freedom,
and sacrifices made by distinctive soldiers.
Now we see the crooked government, corrupt economy,
and our country struggling to improve
Third World problems—poverty, drought, and flood
all need to end and all need a solution.

The Red, White, Blue and Yellow colors of our flag
I am proud of being myself, a Filipino.
We Filipinos must be independent for our future
we as a family, one country,
need to be independent for the community and for ourselves.

MY MOTHER'S WHITE RICE

Ling Hung Young

It was winter,
hot water boiling,
I heard the shush inside the hot pot
as my Mom poured the rice
into the pot,
and the rice started to dance up and down.
I heard the sound lock-lock-lock,
when I looked down into the pot
the water was gone forever,
the rice had gone to sleep.
When I first took one spoonful
and closed my eyes as I ate,
I could feel the flavors of my mom's love.

SON OF THE PHILIPPINES

Mhilz Ang

I am a son of the Philippines
Where my grandmother still lives in a Green Paradise Hill
Where my grandmother enjoys her life
Where my grandmother can water her plants.

I am a son of the Philippines
Where my grandmother shares her heart
Where the birds dance at the morning blue
Where the air whispers in her ear.

I am a son of the Philippines
Where my ancestors talk with the heart of the land
Before the land was taken by the Spaniards
Before the land was crying with blood
Before my people fought back and claimed the lands back
And won the crying land and the rare plants that bloom at night
And plants that only grow in a warm place like our Philippines.

I am a Son of the Philippines
Where people are full with pride
Where a city of people are a family
Where people talk with the heart of the land.

artwork: Andrew Rai

A Mom Present and Awake for Her Children

Epha Ngoy (in honor of my mother)

I'm a strong woman, I'm the window of my family,
because I have to be present
even in midnight if they need me.
I'm a mother, a happiness of my daughter,
I'm a mother, a joy of my sons,
I'm someone who loves to laugh and to have fun,
I'm an amazing African woman for showing my daughter
a good example and making her an independent woman.
I'm a good mother for my sons for helping them
to become good men, independent men.
I'm a happy and proud mom of my kids
who came to America so I could find a good life for my family.
I know very well who my daughter is
and who are my sons.
I'm someone who likes to talk too much
and loves more space for myself.
I'm someone who doesn't like people to touch my kids,
I'm the proud Mom of Epha, Johnson, Jeannot and Jeoffrey.

Ramatoulaye Barry

MY MOTHER

Ramatoulaye Barry

The voice of the Imam from Fajr is the alarm in my home.
Everyone wakes and walks out of their room
looking for the tap and the plastic kettle to find water,
the ablution with natural cold water at four am,
the water splashing on your face
like the stars spinning in the sky at night
wakes you up, and gives you energy.

My Mother

She doesn't need the voice of the Imam to wake her
she doesn't need the cold water to give her energy
everything is in her head like a school's calendar,
she is the strongest woman who exists in this world.
She wanted to see herself in me
her bravery, and her love for Islam in me.
She wanted me to have these characteristics, her characteristics.
She wanted to see me just like the other children in the Mosque
reading the Quran early in the morning.
She wanted to see me looking for the tap and taking my ablution at four am.

But I Was a Disappointment

It's 8 am and I am still in my bed, my class started at 8 am.
I can hear her strong and energetic voice from far away
calling me, "DJIWO."

My Mother

She walks through my room and says,

"Djiwo, open your eyes,
raise your head,
look at the sun walking with your friends
on the way to school,
did you see the moon saying goodbye to your friends,
when they were coming back from the Mosque?
Not at all, because you were so busy, satisfying Sheytan.
Dear Djiwo, the time has no brakes,
it's not going to stop and wait for you,
my daughter, why are you so lazy,
why you don't want to satisfy God, instead of Sheytan?"
She kept saying to me these words, every single day,
over and over, she was never tired
of coming through my room
and repeating these words every morning.

"Girl, you are so lazy,"
took away my confidence,
and made me lazy for real.
I didn't know what I could do,
all I knew was what I could not do.
Everyone called me by the same name,
the same that my mother called me,
Djiwo hi na Ami,
but was I really lazy, or was lazy just stuck in my head?
Because today I can do the same duties as my friends,
I am as brave as them.

Morally, I was lazy, but physically I was strong.

To My Mother

I do realize that I am not lazy,

I do realize that you care about me,

that you wanted me to be a good person.

It took me many years to realize that

you wanted me to succeed, because

the success was not me lying in my bed.

For My Mother

I learned how being organized is important in my life.

I learned how to satisfy God instead of Sheytan.

I learned how to be a good Muslim.

Mother, you're an example to me and I am grateful to you.

FAR FROM HOME

Wasim Azizi

I am far from my mom
I am far from that love
which is sweeter than *halwa*,
the sweetest bread
baked for hours by the hands of those
who carry on the ancient tradition.

I am far from the support that encourages me
to be a different person, different
than I would have become if I had stayed
home in Afghanistan.

I am far from the spicy *shorwa*
and all of the times my mother stirred the pot
with the bright smell that showed the love
of my mom, bright like her mind,
strong, like her actions.

I am far from the song
my mom sang to me
Ah la lo la lo,
the lullaby that relaxes me,
that comforts me and puts me to sleep.

I am far from all of these things,
these things that make me absent
from my life, from my everything,
I am far from my life.

MEMORIAS DE NIÑA

Cecilia A. Cruz Ortiz

I wish I could remember the warm arms of my grandma,
how she hugged me before going to sleep.
I wish I could remember the taste of food my abuelita made,
the *tamales que saben caídos del cielo.*
Ese olor que llega hasta el segundo piso de la casa, ese olor que despierta el apetito.
I wish I could remember the National Anthem (Himno Nacional) from Mexico.
Why can't I remember!!!!
I will not forget the sadness I felt when I last saw my mom, that feeling
that was killing me from the inside.
I will not forget the last goodbyes to my family,
that feeling that broke my heart!!!
Why, why can't I forget!!!

MY HOMELAND IN KENYA

Najmo M. Abdi

I remember my cousin little Faduma and me giggling
and having a good time like sadness never existed in our souls.
I remember the big old tree that was in our house in Kenya
and the blue bright shiny sky.

I remember when I had to leave my homeland and my friends,
and every little mistake I made from the day I was born,
why can't I forget all the times I failed?

I will never forget my country Kenya, and the picture I see
of the tall white mosque, the chief calling the prayer.

I remember when my big sister and I would leave the crowded city,
we would walk miles and miles in the dry sun,
into the deep, earthen red desert,
how tired we were, the sweat pouring from our foreheads.

And I remember the smell of my grandmother, like fresh ginger,
the hot, fresh shower in my grandmother's house.
I remember when my grandmother would dress in all white
a white dress and white scarf.
I remember the smell of the fresh cookies
she would bring for her grandchildren,
and the smell of her hot, fresh tasty cake
that would make our stomachs grouchy.

I remember the honey tree that was in my grandmother's house,
and the one day the whole neighborhood came out
and took the honey out and the people of the village
were sharing the sweetness.

And I will never forget my wishes,
that I wish I could change sorrow to joy,
that I wish I could change civil wars into peace,
that I wish I could change everyone's pain to relief.

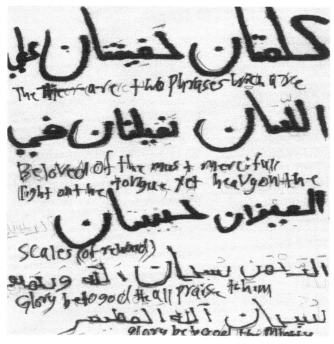

Samsam Hirsi

DAUGHTER OF NEPAL

Salina Biswa

I am the proud daughter of my homeland, Nepal.
I wish I could go back to the sunflowers,
the roses, and the rhododendrons.
I want to return to the Nepali house my dad made,
I want to hear the leaves falling down,
I want to climb the trees outside of my Nepali house
looking high up in the tree for mangoes.
I want to pick the guavas from our guava trees,
I want to run outside in the rain.
I wish I could go to my Uncle's house
and pick the hanging palm berries.
I wish I could go back to my friends,
I wish I could go back to my Auntie.
I am the daughter of Nepal,
I am the daughter of my home.

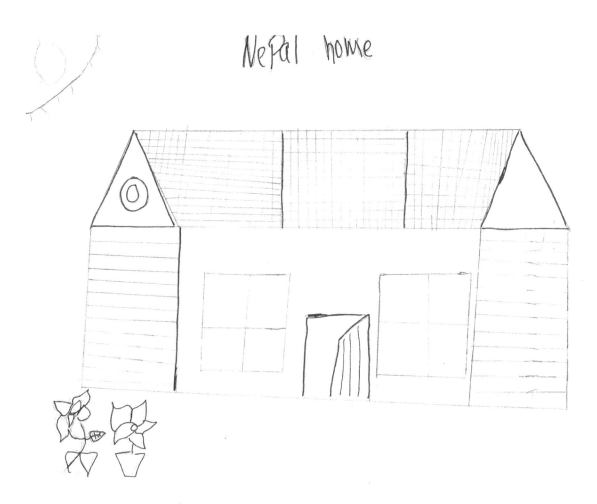

Salina Biswa

FAMILY

Kripen Rai

I remember the houses in my home country Nepal
made of bamboo and bricks built by the strong hands of people
who volunteered to build our community.

I remember the high school students stealing for fun in Nepal,
who would climb up tall trees and steal fruits—mangoes and apples.
And I remember the people who were frequently arrested
for starting fights, for asserting their power.

And I will not forget those who used to help people,
giving them money and supporting their families,
I was always thankful for them.

I hope one day to return to Nepal,
I hope one day I see my family again.

MEMORIES

Jesus Soto Lopez

I remember
when I was in Mexico
celebrating Christmas in my abuela's house,
mi Tio, mi Tia, mis Primos y Primas, y Abuelos y Abuelas.
This happens every Christmas
in Sinaloa, Los Mochis,
I miss this the most
because everybody used to
unite and have a fantastic night.

I remember when me and my grandma
used to play cards and when my brother and I
used to go to an arcade near my grandma's house
and play for hours until we ran out of money.

Why can't I forget when I left my country
and all my friends,
to come to the United States for a better life
for me and my family.

Why can't I forget when my cousin started crying
because my family and I were going to leave
and probably never come back.

My Memories

Carmen J. Hernandez

I remember the sun shining in the morning,
and the shadows entering through the window,
how beautiful the sky looked—orange, pink, grey and blue,
when I woke up, I felt I was in heaven,
like the sun was giving me a massage
and the colors opened my eyes.

I remember the smell of the coffee
in the morning made by my Aunt Erika
the taste of that sweet coffee.

I remember the days
when my family and I celebrated Christmas
and we saw and heard the fireworks
outside my Aunt Erika's house.

I remember when I played soccer
with my cousins outside the house in the yard,
and we spent all day together enjoying
the afternoon, eating ice cream,
seeing how the sun was hiding behind the mountains.

These are the days I tell to myself,
never forget where you come from,
hold all the beautiful moments from my country,
my Honduras.

Carmen J. Hernandez

I CAN'T FORGET MY MOTHER

Thang S. Khual

I cannot forget my loving mother, Nu Nuam
reading the Bible with me,
teaching me not to fear Revelations,
but to prepare for the Rapture.
I cannot forget my compassionate mother, Nu Nuam
who wants me to reach Salvation.
I cannot forget my generous mother, Nu Nuam
her hands working for our family,
planting the vegetables,
corn, garlic and lettuce
under the sweltering Burma sun.
Her hard work brought us here
and now when I think of my life
I can see the faces of those before me,
my loving mother, Nu Nuam,
watching me, and visions of how I lived
in Burma with my grandparents,
laughing, smiling, and living peacefully.
Now I realize that it's a life for me,
back in Burma with my grandparents.
No matter what, I won't ever forget you, Mother,
I hope one day I'll see you again.

Because She Loves Us

Thang S. Khual

From the time I was born to now,
I don't know how to tell how much my mom loves us
and cares about us.
When my dad went to Malaysia,
she looked after us,
she became both mother and father,
she did everything all the men did
and still did what all the women did.

We worked at the farm
planted vegetables
corn, garlic, and lettuce
those three were the only way to make
more money from our farm.
Most people go home when the sun goes down,
but my mom came home when it was dark.

Every time I looked in her eyes
they were always red from a lack of sleep.
I think it's because she thought about us and our life
when she couldn't sleep, then she read the Bible,
she loved to read the Bible more than anything else,

every night she read it with us,
that's the most important in our life.

People don't change, but time has changed,
after we came to the U. S, not even here for a year
and I had to say to my mom goodbye,
I said, "Mom, please read the Bible for me,
even though if I'm a black sheep of the family
you forgive me everything."

Goodbye mother, it's hard to die,
when it's dark and all the stars slowly move
back to their position, I always see you in my mind,
you are coming home from the farm,
I can't stop thinking of you,
I can't wait to see you in a better place.

BALEADAS

Carmen J. Hernandez

My mother's hands rolled the flavor gently
covering the *masa* with water,
pressing the water and the flavor
into a circle, next she waits
for ten minutes,
the right time to make the tortilla.

MY GRANDMOTHER

Sibhat Gebrekidan

I cannot forget my grandmother whose name is Sias Sias
She was born in Eritrea and lived in Eritrea Adi Quala,
She who believed in orthodox religion, she who was a religious person
And she had wishes to have a deacon in her family
And she had six boys including my dad,
And she sent them to St. George Church.

My grandmother wanted all of her boys to learn the Bible and mass and liturgy
But none of those six boys wanted to be deacons,
She felt unlucky, she was always angry and crying and praying to God,
Saying, "Before I die, I want to see a deacon from one of my sons."

I cannot forget that later when I grew up
My grandma chose me to be a deacon,
I told her, "Yes, I can try,"
I started going to church when I was eleven,
I showed a good start and my grandmother was happy,
I can see now how she had big hopes in me.

I cannot forget that after two years at age thirteen
I stopped going to church,
My grandmother was angry and sad,
Even when I said "no" she kept asking
If I would go back to church,

She was disappointed because her wishes
and her dreams did not come true.

Why can't I forget that I was the last person
To make her dream happen, but she did not see her dream,
And a few years ago she passed away,
But I still remember it,
I don't want to remember it,
I want to forget it,
Why can't I forget?

MY MEMORIES

Sahra Hirsi

I will never forget my mother snuggling me in bed
and I will never forget her beautiful voice, her angel voice.
And I will always remember her tasty food,
her delicious rice with the sweet vegetables,
and I will always remember her perfume, honey and rose blossom.

And I will never forget the last time she hugged me,
or the tears coming out from her eyes,
and I will never forget the sadness from her face
or her shouts, calling to me to stay with her.

Tears from Her Eyes

Samsam Hirsi

Why can't I remember
The days that I used to live with my mother
Feeding me and my little sister
Warm *injera*
With her hands
In our home in Somalia.
Why can't I remember waking up next to my little sister.

Why can't I remember
Sarah, Sihaam, Mohamed, Abdul Khadir, and Ayesha.
Why can't I remember walking to school
With my brother and sister
My brother would protest
"I don't wanna go to school."

Why can't I hear the sounds of cooking
The frying of our Somali food,
Anjera mufa,
When my mom cooked.

Why can't I forget the days
I saw my mom's tears pouring
From her eyes saying, "no, please don't leave me,"
Worrying about us because her heart is leaving her.
Why can't I show and tell myself

The strong honest feelings of my mother's heart.
Why can't I forget the beating of her heart.

Why can't I forget seeing my mom's beautiful face,
As she hid her sorrow and anguish
Why can't I forget my mom
As we left unknowingly
For the airport.

I don't want to remember what happened in the past
I want to face the future
I want to hold my mom's hand and tell her,
"Dear mom I am lucky to have you,
Dear mom I have missed you,
Dear mom I love you no matter what."

Pratichya Biswa

I Am a Sister of Janga

Pabi Gajmer

Brother you are always supporting me
the many things you have done
like when you took me to the hospital,
you took care of me when I was afraid,
you took me shopping and spent time with me
all the time you are there to help me.

Deep down inside we know
we always help each other and our family,
I know you, my brother, you carry responsibility for our family,
I know you've taken them to the hospital—mom, aunt and dad,
sometimes at the same time, you manage it all.
Brother, you never worried about your work time,
you just do what makes the family happy.

Brother, I am your sister
I always mean what I ask of you,
and you get angry with me
when I talk too much.
Brother, whenever you come home from work
I never give you a rest,
sometimes I fight with you and talk loudly.

No matter what happens
we will always be sister and brother.
It is my happiness and my pride
knowing we always will be there for each other.

I WANT TO REMEMBER HIM

Monica Hniang Dawt Chin

I want to remember my grandfather Dharkul walking in the garden in Hakha.
I want to remember him.
I want to see him sewing his bamboo baskets for my grandmother.
I want to see him bending over picking his vegetables—
lettuce, chili, carrots, mustard greens and green beans.
But when I try to draw a family picture of him, I cannot imagine him,
I don't remember his face.

Still, I cry every night missing him. I miss sleeping on his chest.
I want to remember him.
I want to remember him staying with my grandmother Chianawn
and working together with her.
I want to remember him telling me stories when I was going to sleep.

He was the one who made me the happiest,
like I was the only person in the world.
I miss him every second, every minute,
every hour and every day.
I remember his last words, "What are you doing with that hammer?"
I want to remember him telling me to always be careful with the hammer.

CHATPATE

Chandra Biswa

When I hear the word *chatpate*
it reminds me of my brown people and my ancient culture
the smell reminds me of my mom's kitchen in Nepal
chilies, tomato, lemon, potato
so spicy, my tongue burns
when I grab a spoon full.
When I think of the word *chatpate*
it reminds me of my country
eating *chatpate* in the rain,
it brings my memories from the past,
with my friends Anisha, Dolma my family
and me having fun, talking to each other while eating *chatpate*.

In Honor of My Father

Chandra Biswa

Being your daughter is a blessing.
You work your whole life just for us.
In early morning I see you working in the shed you built,
Your love is working like a kukuri knife.
You take me to the market
To sell kukuri knives
We set them out,
We play our roles.

The way you show your love is sharper than a knife.
When I am feeling sad, you are there to hold me up,
I am your blood.
You are my blessing, my dad.

BY: Teddy

I need to
make things
with my
hands every day

Happiness in life is in
your own hand

Tewodros Sisay

CURRIES OF MY ROHINGYA KITCHEN

Rujina Bibi Mojullah

When my dad started cooking
the fragrances of the spices,
deep red chilies, finger-staining yellow turmeric,
sharp yet delicate ginger,
these smells moved through my nose
when I walked inside my house.
The spices, curries, and the thick sauces
congregated on the stove,
fish to potatoes, tomato to onion,
onion to red pepper and cilantro
warmed the room with every stroke.
When the spices were in the pot,
they married and bubbled.

My Dear Memories of My Dad

Rujina Bibi Mojullah

Memories of the spicy fish curry with potatoes
the sound of the rain falling
on the plastic sheets that covered our thatch roof,
my father frying onions with all the ingredients
he bought from the market,
and making dinner for us.
Memories of the day I ate fried noodles with my father
and he gave me more noodles from his plate
when I devoured all of mine.
Memories of the time I asked for a noodle package
and he bought it for me
even though he didn't have enough
money to buy food for our family.

Memories of the joy I had
climbing an enormous mango tree,
choosing green mangoes for my family,
and the mango salad my dad made for us,
the taste that was so sour and too spicy.
Memories of the time I spent with him
fishing in the freshwater lake
surrounded by coconut trees and green grass.

(cont)

Memories of the image of my father
when he bought fresh fish from others
and carried that fish to the market
and he sold it sweating and tired
after a long, hard day of work.

Memories of the day my dad was with me
when I was so sick and he told me
everything would be alright,
and the beef curry he made for me
because I was sick.

Memories of the day my father saved money
to buy new heeled shoes for me,
and the sound of his out loud laughing,
and how he made his wiry black hair stay in place
and the way he looked at himself in the mirror.

Memories of the day that my father
told me how to take care of myself
before I traveled to Malaysia without him
when I was ten years old.

Memories of the help that he gave me
and the love he showered on me
when he was with me,
and the way he told me how to respect others,

and how he helped others, and how he bought food
for our family even when he didn't have much money.

Memories of the way he called me
by my middle name "Bibi,"
the way he thought positively about me
the moments he was always there for me
and the warm hug that my father gave me
before I left my village and all of my family.
Memories of the last day and the last time he was with me,
all day without going anywhere
before I had to leave.

How can I ever find the words to say
how much I love my dad, how much I miss him.

MEMORIES OF MYSELF AND MY FATHER

Gavin Dylan Garcia

Will I remember when you stood up to be my father,
the meaningful memories that we made together,
the goals that we wanted to achieve together as a family—have a bright future,
establish a business of having a garage and being a mechanic.

Will I remember that we have the same hobbies,
riding vehicles and exploring untraveled roads,
the beautiful mountains, dusty roads and hilly landscapes
around the Philippines we explored.

Because I will never forget
the day that you left me and my mother,
all the memories we built together, flying away,
and the negative words that you said to us, *Ayoko na sainyo*,
never coming back and you would be remarried again to another woman.

You made my dreams shatter,
you made my soul heavier, and my future darker,
but me and my mother will strive for greatness
and will face everyday problems as a family.

MY FAMILY, MY BHUTANESE PEOPLE

Andrew Rai

I will always remember my family members
and my great grandfather,
and my old house, a small house
made of soil and bamboo
with a small stream near the house
in the refugee camp.

And I will always remember the Bhutanese people
with no place to go
because they are waiting for freedom
in the Nepalese refugee camps.

How, How, How
DID WE GET FROM THE NEPALESE REFUGEE CAMP
TO FREEDOM?

I will always remember the hard and hot sun
that burned you like you were walking in the desert
unable to extinguish the flames
of humidity that happens only in Nepal.

I will never forget that God gave us a second chance.

THE DIVERSITY LOTTERY* BROUGHT US: THINGS MY FATHER TOLD ME

Zulalureman M. Ebro

My father speaks:

One day my friend and I walked on the city street
in Bale Robe in Ethiopia,
we saw a DV Lottery sign in the Internet Cafe,
the U.S. Department of State Electronic Diversity Lottery
that millions of Bale Robe people apply for
hoping to win so that they can leave the broken economy,
$2.00 a ticket can give you the chance of a new life.
We applied
and we won!
I left Ethiopia on February 2, 2009.
I left behind my six children
Zulalureman, Fozia, Asanti, Gutema, Anisa, Hamziya
and my wife Gabi.
And then I moved to the USA.
I could speak English a little, but not fluently.
I couldn't get a job because I was new to the country.
I had no family to help me,
life was hard when I first came to the USA,
no language, no family, no employment.
Then I started my family's case in 2014,

after two years they joined me,
they came to the United States on May 13, 2016.
That moment we reunited
they were walking in the airport
I did not see them,
I did not recognize them,
my daugher Fozia saw me.
My daughter! My daughter! My daughter!
She ran to me,
when she was close to me
and I saw her, my heart was mended.
And then my all family came to me
I felt nearly complete.
I am a hero
because I worked hard to bring my family together.
Alhamdulilah, thanks to God

And this is my father's story of arrival.

* The Diversity Immigrant Visa Program (DV Program) makes up to 50,000 immigrant visas available annually, drawn from random selection among all entries to individuals who are from countries with low rates of immigration to the United States.

MORNING VIEW

Pabi Gajmer

I remember when I was six years old
the view of my village in the morning
sunrise red, a halo above the mountain
reflecting the green of the earth.

Can city people feel the morning view, like we can in the village?
If they feel it, does it make them proud, or are they too busy?
In the morning, village people wake early,
start to pray "Hope my family receives a blessing,"
"Hope our day is great."
One day, I asked dad, "Why do you pray to the morning view?"
Dad told me, "In the morning view, we can see God,
that is why I pray every morning."

Why can't I forget
the morning I looked at the view,
dark this time, making me scared,
I'm so scared of losing myself
in the view, thinking about that moving cloud,
foreboding, alone, afraid it would take me away.
I cried over and over until my dad
heard my crying voice,
he told me that it was just a dark view,

"You don't need to be scared,"
even now, I am too scared
of foreboding skies, worried about clouds
never changing from black.
I hope it will not happen again.

Andrew Rai

REMEMBERING AND FORGETTING

Ahku Kuedituka

Why can't I remember myself growing up in my childhood memories
in Federal Way, dancing, laughing, playing outside, inside, anywhere.

Why can't I remember seeing my dad's brother before his death,
seeing his face when I was a little girl,
now, grown up I cannot see or talk to him anymore.

Why?

Why can't I forget the big orange fire that almost burned down
the La Vista apartments, that scary moment when everyone had to leave
their homes with their children and relatives standing and watching
while the firefighters were coming to save the day.

And why can't I forget my mom's stories
about the Democratic Republic of Congo, how it is unsafe
with dangers to the people and their children,
stories of why she left for America, for safety.

Why can't I forget about the children who are hungry
and the people who have no justice.

Why can't I forget that I'm not like everyone else,
that I'm different too.

Eritrea, My Homeland, My Grandfather

Awet Berhane

I am the son of Eritrea,
I care for the people who are alive in my country now.
I am the son of living in a small village near the Ethiopian border
where my grandfather lived in his small, orange house
that he made from his hands with wood and straw
before he was married.
Every day he ate what he grew,
beans, eggs from our own chickens,
and from the garden he raised he ate his lettuce.
He loved his garden like he loved his children,
he took care of food and people in the same way,
and he was a caretaker of the poor people on this earth,
feeding them, building homes for them.

But I feel sadness for my country, and my grandfather felt sad too,
the government took from him everything we had,
our garden, our money, our feeling of safety.
My grandfather passed away when I was eight years old,
and I will never forget the way he took care of everything around him,
I am still his grandson,
and I am still the son of Eritrea.

'You are everything I could even need and more, more than I deserve or would dare wish for.

ERITEA

Awet Berhane

DEEPA GAVE US A WARM WELCOME when we visited the Namaste Garden.
She delighted in our poems as we placed them around the garden
and then she put us to work!

For more about the Namaste Garden, see page 16.

In Celebration of Gardens Near and Far

artwork:
Thang S. Khual

I remember the hot smell of habanero of my mom's empanada — Josue Tebalan

My Grandmother Will Always Matter

Monica Hniang Dawt Chin

My grandmother's garden in Myanmar is colorful
with peaches, carrots, potatoes, tomatoes,
cucumber, cabbage, celery and green beans.
Her house is old, but surrounded with flowers—
aster, gerbera, pansy, dahlia and poppies.
Her flowers are waving to her.
She is old, but can work as hard as a young woman,
everyone in our village is proud of her.

I am her grandchild and it makes me like I am a queen
of our village, because we were always together, working together.
I want to be with her, my grandmother, and work with her
in her garden like we used to do.

I love helping her, my grandmother, a strong woman
who knew me the best, who taught me different things to grow
and told me some tricks to make them extra delicious.
I still remember the sound of her laugh, soft like a pillow,
how happy she was to have her house and garden.
I want to be with her,
I still remember her young face,
sprinkled with light,
and her long grey hair, like flower stems.

SUNFLOWER

Najmo M. Abdi

You shine like a yellow planet
You shine like the big yellow sun

You sparkle like a diamond in the sky

You sparkle in the fall and look
like a pearl in the summer.

RUNNER BEAN

Nhan Nguyen

I am a runner bean,
Tied to the net so I don't fall,
Can you guess what's inside of me?
I know what it is, but I will not give you
A hint, you have to find out,
I spent my time a-growin!

I remember the sound of the town festival music running through my ears. —Gavin Dylan Garcia

SUNFLOWER
You shine like a yellow planet
You shine like the big yellow sun

You sparkle like a diamond in the sky

You sparkle in the fall and look
like a pearl in the summer.

Najmo, M. Abdi, from Somalia

GREEN ZINNIA

Pabi Gajmer

Zinnia, you are green with leaves
they would grow, reaching
with their long, thin petals
tall and full of summer's brightness
symmetrical flowers filled with attitude
finding comfort and feeling free.

Flower, you are everything to me,
because you make me smile.

ZINNIA

Ling Hung Young

Zinnia, wake up from sleep,
Rise as the sun rises,
Sleep as the sun goes down,
Petals fly like butterflies,
Fall down like rainfall,
Beautiful, like a bride.

Asters / September Flowers

Chandra Biswa & Monica Hniang Dawt Chin

Aster, you remind me of the girls in my dreams
Aster, you smell as good as fresh air in the morning,
Aster, you look like a white angel
Aster, you shine bright as diamonds on Cinderella's slippers
Aster your light blinds me when I look at you.

I remember the taste of the hot rain when I opened the door in the Philippines — *Mhilz Ang*

RED HOT FLAMING PEPPER

Jesfer Lee Agustin

Dear Red Hot Flaming Pepper

Your skin is just like the skin of the old man
who has been worn out through time and experience.

Yet, inside you are a fierce hot seed just like an old soldier,
whose mind and soul has been strengthened by age and experience.

That's why I do not dare to underestimate your spiciness
that can be as hot as the sun.

I remember when my heart felt like a bird. —*Sibhat Gebrekdian*

Epha M. Ngoy

THAI BASIL

Chi Hlaing

Smells like a beautiful woman dancing,
Did the rain encourage you?
Your beauty bothers me.
You're like that one person
I'm always thinking about,
You love the rain when it falls
from the cloud.

PURPLE BEANS

Nasro H. Mohamed

From the galaxy,
Black as night,
Bright as purple flowers,
If I plant you, what magic will happen?

GREEN ZINNIA
Zinnia, you are green with leaves
they would grow, reaching
with their long, thin petals
tall and full of summer's brightness
symmetrical flowers filled with attitude
finding comfort and feeling free.

Flower, you are everything to me,
because you make me smile.

Pabi N. Gajmer, from Nepal

I remember the sound of the deep forest full of the river flowing —Ling Hung Young

ZINNIA

Salina Biswa

Zinnia, growing up colorful and long, growing in the sun,
Zinnias are the reasons for the blooms,
Zinnias are as changeable as water, and happy for the long day
and abundant seeds,
yet, summer skies make no promise
beyond today.

I remember the smell of the wet dirt. —*Jesus Soto Lopez*

Ubah Osman

EL CHILE

Cecilia A. Cruz Ortiz

El chile tan rojo como la sangre que fluye en tu cuerpo.
El chile tan rojo como las flores rojas.
El chile tan rojo como el corazón que está de ti.

The chili as red as the blood that flows in your body.
The chili as red as the red flowers.
The chili as red as the heart that is in you.

PEPPERS

Naing Thang

Peppers hot as the sun
What now?
Maybe this is summer season!
These peppers are also as hot as a volcano!
How? Impossible!
Peppers are really hot as the sun.

African Hot Pepper

Ramatoulaye Barry

You are surely my African hot pepper,
Squiggling like the clouds in the sky,
I wonder if you are transformed
into a cloud,
to fly and find me in America?
I remember you smiling to the shining sun, into my garden.

I remember the taste of tamales my grandmother made with love for the whole family. —Cecilia Cruz Ortiz

A Solution in the Garden

Binda Budhathoki

I have memories
struggles and chaos in my life,
that keep coming through me.

I still remember
how it was solved and what I felt,
the feeling helps to remind me
to live my best life.
Now, the feeling supports me
to think back how I had feelings
and what I did that comforted me.

I am so excited that I found a solution in the garden!
The garden teaches me and solves my challenges.
When I have been to the garden, digging
and throwing away old plants and weeds and dried grasses
it opens my life and gives me knowledge.
In the middle of the digging I came up with a question to myself,
I took responsibility for my life because I felt how much worth there is.
What I saw in the garden were the living, green plants,
I knew that the green encouraged me to be vital.
Being around the plants, and eating them
would keep me healthy and whole with their fresh life.

I remember my mother's hands saying goodbye to me when I was leaving. —Rujina Bibi Mojullah

THE GARDEN OF MY HOMETOWN

Ubah Osman

I remember
the garden outside of my home
in Jigjiga, Ethiopia,
a garden with tomato, onions, garlic,
salad greens, apples, carrots, beetroot,
cherries, mango, melon, lemon,
iceberg lettuce and peppers.

I remember
I would go every morning
to see how the plants were growing.
They were beautiful like jewels growing
out of the dark earth,
every day when the sun came out
and I loved it.

I remember
I wanted to work always in that beautiful garden
smelling like honey and tasting sweet and sour,
and every day colorful and kind.

Beerta ka baxsan guriga ee Jigjiga Itoobiya
beerta leh yaanyo

Basasha, toonta

tufaax, karootada

cherry beetroot Mango, qaraha

liin, lebbiska salad halkas oo aan tagi lahaa subax walba

Si aad u aragto sida dhirta ay u korayaan Waxay ahaayeen kuwo qurxoon,

oo dhammaantoodna way muuqdeen

maalin walba marka qorraxdu soo baxdo

oo aan jeclaa waxaan doonayaa inaan mar walba shaqeeya

beerta quruxda badan oo dhanna waxaa ka soo bixi doona malab

iyo dhaqanka sida maalin kasta

iyo dhanaan leh muuqaal midab leh oo caan ah

I was planted in Thailand, in the land of Bangkok, but blossoming in a refugee camp —Chi Hlaing

SUNFLOWER

Shafi Mohamed Osman, Samsam Hirsi, & Sahra Hirsi

Cover your plant like a mother covers her child,
Raise to the sunshine like people raise a flag to peace,
You look like the sun that keeps the plant growing.
You are colorful like the sun
and the rainbow.

Pratichya Biswa

Cecilia A. Cruz Ortiz

COUNTRYSIDE

Tewodros Sisay

I am a son of Ethiopia
and a son of its trees and forests,
where my grandmother lives in a village in the countryside,
where there are many plants waiting to be found,
and many flowers growing from the ground,
where my grandmother grows tomatoes, potatoes, sugarcane,
a countryside I love because you can see
many different kinds of nature for free.

I am a son of Ethiopia
where nature helps the world to live
by giving a joyful life, natural life,
so we must treat our countryside
with respect, with kbr.

HE WHO MISSES HIS GARDEN

Anass Harma Alaoui

I am the son of Morocco
where my family eats at the same table
eating with their right hands
and sometimes sharing spicy chicken from a Tagine.

I am the son of Morocco
a place where the sun shines
on our orange terracotta house,
where outside my auntie Hayat's house
we have planted a big garden,
a garden I helped plant myself,
a garden with lemons, with red and orange
birds of paradise and orange blossom flowers
that clean your eyes when soaked in water
and placed gently on tired eyes
with a small, fragrant cotton cloth.
And we have Aloe Vera the plant that heals wounds
and shines your hair.

I am the son of Morocco who misses this garden,
where we take old tires that no longer work,
we plant our seeds in the ground,
and when the flowers, trees and plants grow bigger
we stack three tires around each growing plant,

we paint the tires yellow and green,
making our garden beautiful,
protecting our flowers and our trees.
This is how me and my Auntie garden in Morocco.
I miss my Auntie Hayat's garden
where I felt as peaceful as the calm ocean.

I remember the taste of fresh tea leaves —Andrew Rai

PAD KAI PAW, DOE DANCE

Chi Hlaing Tun

Girls dancing in the color of green, white, and gold.
The young men dancing viciously in red, white, and gold
like spices and garlic dropped in the pan full of oil.
The sizzling of the pan sounds like the drummer drumming with excitement.
Girls are cleansed like the Thai basil just washed.

Now the girls are ready to join in with the boys, like the basil dropped in the pan
with spices and garlics.
The basil smells wonderful, like the dancers' coordination of their arms and hands,
feet, and legs.
Meat is dropped in, like the excitement of the audience,
It's like the feeling of the devil, but the taste of heaven,
when oyster sauce, fish sauce, sesame sauce, soy sauce, and salt are added.
They dance in a peaceful goodbye and in a "come again."

We Speak For the Earth

artwork: Mhilz Ang

Mother earth speaking:
People are asking for help. I hear children crying
Children hurting I heard them crying.
Can you make a change?
Let us not corrupt her
Let us protect her
Let us be her savior.

—Chandra, Gavin, Najmo, Pabi and Tewodros

EARTH

Pabi Gajmer

Earth, I want to honor you:
With you I have a home,
a place of sunlight.
We are all here on the earth to help each other,
You show me respect to older people,
You show me the ways I need to learn,
I honor you, and your place in people's hearts.

Earth, I want to apologize to you:
We take you for granted,
We poison your water,
We burn too much gas and we pollute your air,
We create wars and prejudice,
I am sorry we have forgotten where we come from,
Who our mother truly is.

Earth, I want to tell you:
We are proud to live here,
We belong to the earth,
We must remember to respect you.

SKY AND EARTH

Jesfer Lee Agustin

I remember the wrath of the primordial gods of sky and earth
when I hear the terrible storms with the quakes shaking buildings
and hurricanes lifting cars or houses, throwing them randomly,
everywhere causing destruction that tainted the earth.

I remember the taste of grief
when the primordial god of sky turned
the white clouds gray, then cried for it saw the earth's burned forests
and the tarnished beauty of the green land of earth
once full of life, turned into a gray city of metal.

I would like to imagine the past when the primordial goddess of earth
smiled for joy, and caused vast forests of yellow, red, white
and many other colorful flowers to bloom,
while the wind would caress the flowers,
and the primordial goddess of the sky treated the flowers
like precious jewels, for it was her smile of joy
that caused the flowers to bloom.

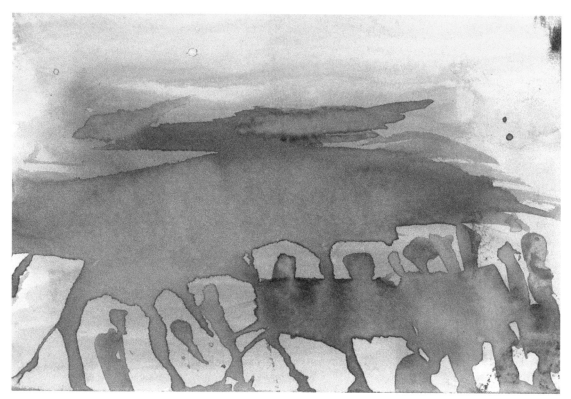

Najmo M. Abdi

Let's make a deal with nature.
You don't know how beautiful it is?!?!
What we do with rivers means they will never come back
because the rivers are angry.
The Earth gave us everything.
One day I hope we can pay her back.

—*Andrew Rai*

This we know that the earth is in need.
She begs us to stop hurting her children.

—*Mohamed Mogow*

Chi Hlaing Tun

The dirt calls for help for us humans to stop what we're doing and change for good.
The Earth is crying because we keep her badly.

—*Jesus Soto Lopez*

The ocean cries because she can no longer sing.
The river dies slowly every day.
The trees cry for help every night while they burn to death.
The earth prays every night her children will grow into good people
who will protect her.

—Najmo M. Abdi

The ocean cares about her children and she is my second mother.
The rain cares about the earth.
He tries to keep the forest from burning and make people comfortable because of him.
Because if the weather is hot and sunny the plants and animals will die.

—Nhan Nguyen

This we know: the earth is in danger
We people must take care of it
For it is where we live
For we deserve a beautiful planet earth.

This we know: the earth gives all of her specialties to us
And now it's time to give some back to her
For we don't want to lose her.

—*Awet, Jesfer, Mhilz, and Mohamed*

The trees are born to be happy
But now have lost their lives
People are greedy and kill them
They take the soul inside the trees
A soul that can no longer grow and change
Then the leaves are shaped like tears as they fall.

—Ling Hung Young

SOUL inside The Trees Soul that Grow and Change The leaves shaped like a tears as They Fall but Live

Ling Hung Young

Our ocean is crying because she cannot sing, why?
The mouth I sing with is full of garbage.
How can I sing?
Our ocean can't give us breath, why?
The ocean is afraid that we might get sick from the bad air.
I am the same ocean, the ocean that used to be everything—beautiful mysterious, wild and free.

— Pratichya Biswa

My Dreams

Najmo M. Abdi

If my heart could speak, it would speak of my dreams,
it would tell you of my solidarity by never giving up
on my dream to become a teacher,
it would speak of injustice in the world
and of civil wars in Somalia.

If my heart could sing, it would sing about the struggles in the world,
young black teens getting killed by police, and #blacklivesmatter,
it would sing about the hunger that lives in our world,
and the hope that hunger will no longer exist.

If my uncle could speak he would say, no matter what happens
always follow your dreams, and accomplish them.
If my uncle could speak he would say,
never hate, always love.

If the earth could talk she would talk about her struggle, pain, and pollution,
she would tell us to take care of her and recycle and not litter,
she would say, I am your home, please take care of me.

THE TREES ARE CRYING

Thang S. Khual

The trees are crying
They are saying, "Why are we being destroyed?"
The trees are disappearing,
The weather has changed,
There are no longer birds singing sweetly in the trees,
When I look down from a lofty mountain grandeur,
I am not hearing the singing brook,
I am not feeling the gentle breezes.

Andrew Rai

LIFE OF VIETNAM

Nhan Nguyen

Does my heart remember?
Fishing to catch food
in the beautiful ocean Bai Tay,
the hot orange sunlight
burning my skin,
swimming in the deep blue ocean near Nha Trang
feeling like walking to Paradise.

Does my heart remember?
Eating sweet mango
wrapped in speckled green skin.
Mango tree is like a human,
has a life and has a name
Hoa Loc, Xoai Xanh...
Mango has 35 species,
thinking that speckled green mango may not be sweet
but if I try it, I want to devour all of the mango,
tastes like sugar or sweet candy,
holding mango in my hand
like I was holding a black five pound weight.

Does my heart remember?
My thinking is broken piece by piece,

I'm feeling heavy when I taste
little mistakes in my red heart.
I was thinking my grandfather was the mango tree,
not sweet, let this thinking get out of my brain
the word "sorry" almost runs out of my mouth.
Forget it!

Will I forget?
Garbage piling up,
alcohol bottles and plastic food containers on the street
take over with the rotten smell of mouse urine.
All flowers have colors: red blood, light pink,
purple mixed with black,
like all sidewalks have colors with people,
light brown skinned people like me,
but everything beautiful is turning to dark grey,
the fragrance of flowers has gone away,
can no longer smell the flowers
planted on the road that I go through daily,
the stench of garbage was pushing them away,
smoke of motorbikes flying to the beautiful white sky,
changing to dark and grey,
making the mad rain come,
but it never happens.

And that is life in my country Vietnam.

The moon puts her blanket over the sun every night.

Mohamed Mogow

I SPEAK FOR MYSELF AND FOR THE EARTH

Mohamed Mogow

I speak for myself to be myself
to be a respectful young man,
to respect my family
to respect all animals
and to respect people all over the world
no matter their skin color, race or religion.

I speak for the Earth
and its beautiful landscapes
that people live in,
for the amazing animals
that live on earth and in water,
for the powerful volcanoes
that erupt lava,
for the salty oceans
that spread from one continent to another,
and for the tall, beautiful, living trees
that give humans breath.

I speak for the people who have gardens
on their land, stretching all over the continents,
I speak for the earth,
for her sons and her daughters.

NEPALI RIVER

Pratichya Biswa

Our river is crying because she cannot sing.
> How can I sing when my own people used my mouth
> as a place to hold garbage—bora, papers, vegetables,
> fruits, plants, and banana trees.
> How am I supposed to sing?
> I don't want to give you a breath.

Why?
> I can't give you breath

Why?
> Because I am afraid that you might get sick of that bad air.

> Why are you making me cry?
> I am the same river who would move freely.
> I used to be everything for my people, beautiful, wild and free.
> But when people started to throw things in me
> they changed me to...

> Why did you change me to this? Why?
> People throw maila—empty bottles, plastics for food packaging,
> worn clothes, metal.
> These things are disgusting.
> Now, those same people don't even want to come next to me.

Why?
> Because I am not the same as the one before.

Why?

Because of you, they don't know that I used to be
a safe home for swimmers, for children, for all of us.

Why are you ignoring me?
I am calling you to come next to me
to make me the one I was before.

Let me sing again,
let me be beautiful again,
let me be free again,
let me be near you again,
and listen to my song,
and see my beautiful clear waters
and I will stop crying.

THE DRY EARTH

Samsam Hirsi

The tree is looking at me with his sad eyes full of tears.
If I look at him I'll cry too.
Let me ask you, where are your fresh green innocent leaves?
They have been taken away from me.
Where are your strong and long branches?
They have been taken away from me.
By what?
The drought, the dry earth.

Jesus Soto Lopez

THE LAND IS CRYING

Chi Hlaing Tun

Do you hear that?
He's crying, the land is crying.
Without him, our animals and our food, we wouldn't be able to live.
His sister is polluted, his brother is also polluted.
We humans are selfish, we think for ourselves and not about what's around us.
Our nuclear waste is killing him.
Our conflicts are also killing him with our wars.
Do you still hear him?
Or are you just blind and deaf?
Because we are also killing ourselves.
But let us be human and love our surroundings.

Anass Harma Alaoui

CHILDREN OF MOTHER EARTH

Jesfer Lee Agustin

We are children of Earth.

We are children of this emerald land
liquid sapphire ocean known as Earth.

We are children who live on her emerald land filled with beautiful
brown trees, yellow and red flowers, standing tall, rooted deep within her.

She who gives us warm yellow fire in the dark quiet night
as the shadows silently creep into our hearts,
shifting into our fears.

She who fills the world with beauty and wonders for us
to view under the comforting blanket of the sun.

She who has been there for our time of need
needs our help, because her vast green forests
are withering through fire,
and her once clear, sparkling, sapphire waters
are now polluted by vile trash and chemicals.

We her children notice her pain and cries through the rain and dark clouds.

We will help heal her in her time of need
for she helps us in ours.

We who notice Mother Earth's pleas for help, this is for you.

Nhan Nguyen

WE BELONG TO THE EARTH

Kripen Rai

We have to pick the garbage up and drive fewer cars.
We have to walk more and care about the earth.
As chief Sealth reminds us,
We belong to the earth
All things are connected, like the blood which unites one family
All things are connected.
We have to care for the earth like we care about our Mother.
We have to make her happy and proud of us forever.

Dear Human

Ramatoulaye Barry

Our Mother the Ocean,
our Father the Earth
care about us
but do we care about them?
The animals, our brothers and sisters
are devastated by our actions.

Dear Human they are our responsibility,
they are our family,
we are meant to be a single neighborhood in this world.
So, let me ask again,
are we taking good care of the ocean, the earth and the animals?
Because it seems like only our lives matter in this world.

Dear Mother Ocean,
of all living things in the world
I'm Sorry to see you so sad
because we Humans degrade you day by day,
leading to the gradual disappearance of your fauna, and flora.
I'm Sorry to see your children "the animals,"
hurt in front of your eyes in your home
because of the huge amounts of toxic waste and wastewater
that are released into your environment.

Dear Father,
of all living things in the world

I REGRET that your children, "Humans," have disappointed you
by the application of weapons, the military transport movements for wars
and the spraying of chemicals on the earth for their own reasons.
I REGRET that the children you bore are hurting you
by the destruction of your landscape to drill their oil fields,
and the wildfires they caused for their greed.

Dear Human being
Canvas gives us home,
Kitchen gives food,
Work gives money,
Bed gives rest,
Life gives pleasure,
Water gives life,
Animals give love,
and Earth,
the Earth gives everything.

We all can do something to save our Mother and Father
because one good action is never a little action
and doing nothing and remaining silent does not help.
One voice will not go far,
one arm will not reach,
but together, we are strong, together we will raise our voices,
we will stand strong for the only home we have.

We are all from different nations, but we all are equal.
We all live under the same sky and we all are in one family
who live on one earth.
We should care, share, and love each other.

Ling Hung Young

THANK YOU

TO OUR LONGSTANDING PROJECT PARTNERS who have been the bedrock of our support since the inception of the project.

JOAN RABINOWITZ, *Executive Director of Jack Straw Cultural Center, Seattle*

Each year, our students record poems in Jack Straw's state of the art studios and receive attentive and expert individual voice coaching. The poems are broadcast on KBCS 91.3 FM every weekday of April in honor of National Poetry Month. Joan Rabinowitz, Executive Director of Jack Straw Cultural Center, has been a key supporter of our poetry project, along with her amazing crew of voice coaches and sound engineers. Joan's extraordinary vision for bringing diverse voices and art forms to Seattle, King County and beyond has increased the cultural presence of numerous and highly varied groups of all ages enriching our city and county by celebrating a multiplicity of artistic and cultural life. The generous financial support that accompanies the voice coaching, recording and production of our students' poetry is a centerpiece of our project. Find additional information about the Stories of Arrival Project in partnership with Jack Straw Cultural Center and recordings of our students' poems at www.jackstraw.org.

JOHN FOX, *Founder of the Institute for Poetic Medicine (IPM) in Palo Alto, CA*

The IPM has provided generous financial support for the project, as well as lending a national aspect to our work as an IPM Poetry Partner Project. We are among several poetry projects in the U.S. supported by the IPM who are fortunate in our affiliation with John Fox's nationally and internationally recognized work for using poetry as a healing force in many settings including prisons, hospitals, hospices and shelters for the homeless. As John aptly writes: *There is magic and power in language that poets, children, mystics, lovers, people with broken hearts, revolutionaries, and indigenous people have had access to for eons, and their lasting words have inspired others. Writing and listening to poetry shows a spiritual resilience within and helps us join with a kind of beauty and meaning in life.* John's knowledge of the power of poetry to provide comfort in times of loss and trauma, and to offer praise for what gives us joy, has gifted us with a depth of friendship and wise counsel. Find additional information about the Stories of Arrival Poetry Project in partnership with the IPM and articles in the IPM Journal at www.poeticmedicine.org

WE ARE ALSO GRATEFUL FOR FUNDING from **King County 4 Culture, the Satterberg Foundation** and the **Tukwila School District,** without whom this project would not be possible.

IN ADDITION, WE THANK **Joziah Cladoosby** for his assistance, **Janelle Jordan** and **Laura Gamache** for their mentorship during our revision process, and **Tyler George-Minetti**, **Kamal Adhikari** and **Deepa Iyer** of the IRC New Roots Program for their collaborative spirit and welcome to the Namaste Garden.

AND FINALLY, OUR IMMENSE THANKS TO: **Rachel McDonald,** Young Adult Librarian, KCLS, Tukwila Branch; **Richard Rogers,** graphic designer, for his generosity and support of our project; **David W. Lynch,** photographer extraordinaire for his years of spirited friendship to our project and his generosity of time and artistry; and **Annie Brulé,** gifted book designer, for once again shepherding our book to life with her over-the-top devotion to our project.

About the Poets
Biographies and Portraits

Wasim Azizi

Ahku Kuedituka was born in Tukwila and has lived there for fourteen years. She speaks English and a little bit of Lingala, a language spoken in the Democratic Republic of Congo. Ahku loves dancing, singing, using her phone, and watching TV. Her mom says that the DRC is not a safe place because the president is commanding his soldiers to kill Congolese children and people. So, to live safely, now Ahku's family lives here. When older, Ahku wants to be a software designer for phones for Apple.

Ahku believes that more justice needs to be created and that hungry children who experience starvation around the world should be served. She understands that they deserve more than just a small bite of food and that some children work all day and do not have enough to eat.

Anass Harma Alaoui was born in Morocco at Kenitra. He moved to the USA when he was fourteen years old. He speaks and understands French and Arabic. Anass dreams of graduating and becoming a soccer player; so therefore, he will try his best to reach his dreams. He misses his family and his auntie's cooking with her magic hands. Anass believes that people in Morocco are like brothers and sisters. He misses his country and he wants to go back and live there.

Andrew Rai is fifteen years old. He was born in Nepal and arrived in the USA when he was fourteen. He came to the USA because his family needed to make a better life. In Nepal there is no freedom and no good health care; infrastructure is poor, and even though Andrew was born in Nepal, he never would have been allowed citizenship. He misses his country, his friends, his school and the mountains. He speaks Nepali, Hindi, and a little English. He dreams of graduating.

Andrew misses his country's views every day. He wants to go and see them and feel them because there is no other view like in Nepal. He also misses his culture's food because the food from his country is the best underground cultural food for him and even tastes better if his whole family is cooking it. Even more than the food, Andrew misses his work with the team of people in his country who cared for and tended the plants and trees. This community was called the Plant Server Team (P.S. T.), and Andrew worked hard with them and cared for and saved many plants and trees.

Andrew believes he can make the environment better by saving trees and plants. And he thinks that one day all the people in the world will come to understand the value of the environment.

Awet Berhane was born in Eritrea. He moved to Ethiopia when he was ten years old. He lived in an Ethiopian refugee camp for six years. He arrived in the U.S. in 2015. He can speak Tigrinya, Amharic, and English. He can also speak Geez, mostly at Church. He misses his country's land in Asmara where the streets are clean and friendly. Life in the refugee camp was better than life in Eritrea because there was food and more freedom. Awet dreams of a world where people live in peace and care about each other and the earth.

Binda Budhathoki was born in Nepal and lived there until she was twelve years old. Binda speaks Nepali and English. She likes marigold flowers and her favorite color is pink because it is bright and clear. Binda likes to drink tea, read books, play badminton and support her family by doing chores and taking responsibility. She has six family members.

She loves her country and has many memories of the landscape. Each year she was there she loved celebrating the cultural festivals and she hopes to return to Nepal and see the beautiful temples. Binda likes to be in green places with trees where she gets energy and feels vital. She is curious about learning and wants to do well in school and get more knowledge.

Carmen J. Hernandez was born in Honduras. She lived in Honduras for twelve years and moved to the USA when she was thirteen years old. She came to the USA for a better future and to complete her dream of becoming a doctor. She can speak English and Spanish. Carmen loves to play soccer with her family and spend time together with them. She misses all of her home country: rivers, school, gardens, friends, food, and family. Someday she hopes that she can go back to her country. She also hopes to make her parents proud of her.

Carmen thinks people should plant gardens, be together, and not cut down the trees. Instead, she believes that people should plant and protect them.

Cecila A. Cruz Ortiz was born on February 22, 2001, in Mexico City. She remembers very little, but she says that Mexico is a crowded place and very noisy. She was only nine years old when she moved to the USA. Her mother wanted to move to the USA for a better future because in Mexico education is expensive. Cecila speaks Español. She believes Español is a way to be closer to her culture. To protect the *terra* she believes that people have to be more sensitive to the *terra* by planting more trees, and by cleaning our air. She believes we can also help by replacing what we have destroyed of the *terra*.

Chandra Biswa was born in Nepal; she lived in Nepal for twelve years and then moved to U.S in 2013. She can speak Nepali and English. She loves dancing, listening to music and playing sports. She dreams of helping her family by buying a home where they can live happily. She dreams to become an Air Hostess. Her family came to the U.S. because they wanted to get a better future and education. Her parents wanted more freedom for their children than they had because her parents never went to school. She misses her Nepal, the place where she was born and she misses her cultural foods.

Chi Hlaing Tun was born in Bangkok, Thailand. He was raised in a refugee camp for four years until he moved to America. He can speak three languages, which are English, Karen, and Poe Karen. Chi Hlaing loves cars, and he loves to cook food from Thailand because he loves Thai food. One of his favorite Thai foods is called "Pad Kai Paw." He also loves to cook for his church. He is competitive so he likes to play sports, like Frisbee. His father wanted him to do well in school and in life after his mother died. That's why his father is so strict. His best friend, Jesse, is very encouraging in a hard way.

Chi Hlaing came to America because his parents wanted him and his sister to have a better education. His sister is thirteen. Chi Hlaing gives her tough love. He really misses his friends; where he lived was a beautiful, memorable place. He wishes that he could go back because when he left that place he also left behind his memories. The memories that he hasn't forgotten are the memories of he and his brothers playing soccer, and getting into fights just for fun. He wishes he could go back and do this, but he can't. He didn't know what happened to one of his brothers, so his family contacted the people back in Thailand to see if he was alive. He found out that his brother was still alive so he wishes to go back and see him. They haven't seen each other in a long time. Chi Hlaing's brother is in Thailand with his wife and children. When Chi Hlaing was fifteen he noticed several wonderful things about himself.

Epha M. Ngoy came to the USA from Congo in the big city of Kinshasa in May, 2016. In many places of Africa, people live in bad situations: war, poverty, discrimination, and lack of resources and employment. She came here because she doesn't want to live like that. She has always dreamed of becoming a star in music and becoming a heroine in movies. If she has the opportunity, she'd like to tell her mother's story because it is tragic and resilient. She believes that people can have a better life by loving each other, and by listening to and understanding each other. She is an accomplished singer and has sung in Congo Brazza, Côte d'Ivoire, Senegal, Cameroon and Guinea Conakry.

Gavin Dylan Garcia was born in the Philippines in a little town called Camiling in the province of Tarlac. He was fourteen years old when he came to the U.S. He speaks three languages which are Tagalog, Ilocano and English. He and his family came to the U.S. to have a better future. Gavin didn't just come here to the U.S. to look cool or be cool, his family came here for a bright future. The hard work his family has done to get to the U.S. was worth it. But, being away from their "real home" was hard especially because Gavin grew up in the Philippines and that's where he learned most of what he knows. Gavin misses the smell of fresh vegetables like *Upo, Kamatis and Malunggay*. He also misses his friends and his other family left in Camiling. He also misses the rocky brown roads left by his family's ancestors, the smell of fresh air like expensive cologne, these he misses the most.

For Gavin, protecting the earth starts with ourselves and our surroundings before we go out and help others. Gavin wants to be independent which he thinks is a good start in protecting the earth. When he was a child he dreamed of a world where a community helped each other, where no people were struggling, and where no people were homeless. He always dreamed of a world where everyone was equal.

Jesfer Lee Agustin was born in the Philippines. He lived in Dau for eleven years and he spent time in Tarlac before moving to Seattle in 2011. He can speak several Filipino languages and English and he would love to learn other Asian languages. He loves to play and read. His favorite class is math. Jesfer believes that far in the future technology will be so advanced that we will find a way to live out of the earth's land; during those times of living elsewhere, the earth will hopefully heal itself.

Jesus Soto Lopez is fourteen years old. He was born in Los Mochis Sinaloa, Mexico. He was ten years old when he moved to the USA. His family moved to the USA to find a better life for themselves and their children. Jesus really misses his country; what he misses the most are his grandma and his friends from Mexico and his old house. He made it through life because of them and they helped him become the person that he is now. One of his dreams is that the earth will not be polluted in any kind of way. Another dream Jesus has is to make his family proud and to become successful.

Josue Tebalan was born in Seattle. When he was one year old his dad took him and his sister to Guatemala for one year. Then the next year his mom took them to Veracruz, Mexico. For the next few years, he lived in both countries because his mom is from Mexico and his father is from Guatemala. Josue speaks both English and Spanish. When he finishes high school he wants to go to the Army, or be a doctor in the US. He wants to build seven houses in Guatemala and rent them to make money for his family. He wants to have a rancho in Mexico and have cows, horses, dogs, chickens, sheep, and pigs. He believes having an education will make him successful.

Krinsuk Rai is fourteen years old. He was born in Nepal in a city called Kathmandu. He was ten years old when he came to the USA. He and his family came here to find a better life. He speaks three languages; Nepali, Hindi, and English. He went to school in Kathmandu before they moved to another city. The things he misses are his house and his friends.

Kripen Rai was born in Nepal. He came to the United States when he was nine years old. He came to the U.S. with his brother, sister, and mother. His family migrated here for a quality education, but he misses his family that is still back in Nepal. Kripen has learned to speak two languages, Nepali and English. He desires to stop wars and he dreams of a peaceful world where everyone can live happily. Kripen also likes to play basketball, the position he plays is point guard. When he grows up he wants to be a professional basketball player. He wants to help people who need help.

Ling Hung Young, age fourteen, was born in Mindat, Chin state in Burma. She lived in Mindat for only five years before moving to Malaysia in 2009. Ling's father moved to Malaysia before her whole family came, and then her father sent money to her mother for their essential survival because in Chin state of Chang they don't have jobs to get money, even though they have their own farm which is not enough for them. Ling's mother wanted to move to Malaysia because beside the money issue, she couldn't take care of five children on her own. Ling and her siblings were really excited to move to Malaysia, but after they arrived in Malaysia in July 29, 2009 they started to miss their own country.

On their way to Malaysia it was not easy for them to find safe passage and it took them a month. Ling was five at the time, and therefore the journey had the most dangerous circumstances for her. She walked with her family all the way from her country to Malaysia, being careful along the way. Mostly they escaped at night because they didn't want to be caught by police and soldiers. This was especially hard for her mother, who carried her younger brother who was three years old at the time all the way on her back. Ling remembers wishing that she could help her mother, but there was no way. Many more people from other states joined them, which made the amount of food to feed everyone not enough. Although they struggled on their way, they all arrived safely in Malaysia on July 29, 2009.

Because of these experiences, Ling now believes that we all should take care of each other because there is no one else to take care of us in the world. We are all from different nations, but we all are equal. We all live under the same sky and we all are in one family who live on one earth. We should care, share, and love each other.

Mhilz Ang was born in the Philippines on Cebu Island. He is fifteen years old. He was fourteen years old when he came to the U.S. Mhilz came to the U.S. for better education and to reunite with his family and to have a healthy future. Only his aunt's family is still waiting for their visas to come to America. Mhilz can speak four languages: Filipino, English, Chinese and Cebuano. Mhilz misses his mom's cooking because his mom's *Palabok* tastes like a potion of paradise and always lightens his mood up whenever he feels down.

Mhilz Ang believes that you can be what you want to be as long as you work hard for it and make healthy choices throughout your journey to achieving your goals. When Mhilz was a child there were so many trees around him when playing with his friends. But, when he grew up there were fewer trees and many buildings. Mhilz Ang also believes that if we could just get rid of pollution and stop illegal logging and other bad things that we do to nature, we could make Mother Earth healthy again.

Mohamed Mogow was born in Nairobi, Kenya. He arrived in America in 2008 when he was six years old. Mohamed can speak Somali and English fluently and he is now learning to speak Arabic. He dreams of graduating and becoming a professional soccer player. What he misses about his country are Acacia trees, there are no other trees like them in the world. The wild ferocious animals, the blazing hot sun and the sandy soccer fields of Nairobi that kids play in every day are what he misses most. He also misses his grandmother's cheerful hugs.

Mohamed wants to go back to Kenya after he finishes studying at the university. He doesn't like America and its new rules so much and he wants to take what he learns in the U.S. and return to Kenya to work and to help his country. He is a very active person; his favorite hobbies are soccer, watching movies and playing video games. He doesn't like to sit too long without moving or doing something active. Back in Kenya, Mohamed used to go outside every day and play with his friends. He misses chasing the cows to pass the time.

Monica Hniang Dawt Chin was born in Hakha, Chin State in Burma. She lived in Hakha for eleven years and moved to Malaysia in 2012. She came to Seattle in 2014. She speaks three languages, Hakha, English and Burmese. She is Christian. Monica's dream is to become a model and a singer.

She came to the U.S. because her parents want her to have a better education and to have more freedom. In Burma, the government doesn't give the people enough water, electricity or food. Also, there is a war. Monica misses her country and her garden. Someday she hopes to go back to her country. She thinks people should protect the earth because the earth is like our mother. Monica dreams of a world where she doesn't have to worry about her grandmother, who still lives in Hakha. She hopes her grandmother will live for a longer time so she can see her again.

Naing Thang is fourteen years old. He was born in Burma. He lived in Burma for five years and then moved to Malaysia in 2009. He came to the USA in 2014. He speaks three languages; Malaysian, Burmese, and a little English. The things he misses about his past country, Burma, are: landscapes of mountains, villages, cities, lakes, and his loved people. Naing Thang never went to school when he was in Burma and Malaysia. Now in America, Naing Thang is learning English although he is having a hard time learning it because he's new to America. He didn't go to school at all when he was a kid. In class, Naing Thang doesn't often talk or speak, because he is too shy and scared. But, one year later Naing Thang is learning how to read or write a little by speaking and writing in his new-comer class. New-comer class is a place where a person like Naing Thang learns new things like animals, people, countries, and names of things new to them. Naing Thang has made some new friends now, and along with them he works as hard as he can.

Najmo M. Abdi was born in Kenya in Africa. She lived in Kenya for seven years then moved to the USA. She can speak Somali and English. She loves to help others when they need a hand to lean on. Her family always tells her to pursue her dreams. She loves to help her siblings with their homework and learn new things.

When Najmo looks at the stars she believes anything is possible and that there's a lot we don't know. One day, she wants to be a scientist. Najmo always prays that her dreams will come true. Najmo wants to travel all around the world and help refugees like herself. And one day, she will adopt kids from all around the world and celebrate their differences. Najmo dreams of a world where there are no stereotypes and people do not die of hunger.

Nhan Nguyen came to the United States when he was ten years old. His family left Vietnam for a better life, a good job and to find a good community. Nhan misses many things about Vietnam—New Year's celebrations, his grandfather's mango tree, his country's foods, his family and the heat and busyness of his country. He hopes to see his grandparents and his friends this summer in Vietnam.

Nhan wishes his grandparents could always stay young and wait for him to come back. He really wants to see his dog and he wishes he could bring his dog to the United States. He and his dog were always together like best friends. Nhan dreams of becoming a basketball player. In Vietnam he often talked in class and only sometimes was a good student, but when he came to the United States he wanted to be first at his school, get good grades and make his parents proud of him.

Nhan always remembers his country in his heart and never loses these memories. He hopes people will protect the earth because the earth is our mother and we should respect her as her children. He also believes we should protect the earth like we would care for our parents. Nhan's dream is that wars will no longer happen, but he worries they will never end.

Pabi Gajmer was born in Nepal. She moved to the U.S. in 2011 when she was nine years old. She can speak and understand Nepali, Hindi and English. Her family came to the U.S. for a better education, a better life, and for freedom and changes in their lives. Pabi dreams of helping old and poor people because sometimes old and poor people don't have a place to live and to eat. She feels bad about people who hate and yell at each other. Pabi wants to make a house for poor people to live in and she wants to make them feel better.

Pabi thinks about protecting the earth and she thinks that people should follow laws and rules for protecting the earth and that sometimes people try to break the laws and do whatever they like to do. She thinks people should get together to advocate for change because there needs to be laws that help everyone. She misses her country such as the sound of family and friends in the morning getting ready for school with excitement. She also misses walking with friends at night and talking loudly. She misses the place where she ate *chatpata, momo* and *chow mein*. She is thankful that she doesn't have to live on small food rations anymore like she did in the refugee camp in Nepal. Pabi is hopeful that one day we will never hear of people dying of hunger.

country, Nepal, she misses her garden in front her house growing *chate* and *dalle khursani-chili*, the spiciest chili in all of Nepal. In Nepal everyone speaks the same language and talks about their gardens and what to grow next.

Pratichya lives with both of her parents. Her dad never wrote any poems, but her dad's life was poetry without using any ink! Her mom is not that educated, but she always helped with her children going to school and getting a bright future. Pratichya dreams that all children would have parents and a safe place to live just like our Mother Earth gives us a safe place to live.

Ramatoulaye (Rama) Barry is a young African woman. She was born in Guinea Conakry in West Africa. She has the same culture as all the Fula people of Guinea, one of the most ancient and largest ethnic groups of Africa. She is seventeen years old. She went to Sierra Leone when she was twelve and came back at thirteen. She spent her childhood between her village Dalaba and in the city of Conakry. At the end of 2015, she went to Senegal and moved to the U.S at the age of sixteen. She speaks Foulani, French and English. Ramatoulaye is a Muslim believer and her religion is part of her identity. Today she is worried about what is going on in the world

Pratichya Biswa was born in Nepal. She was thirteen years old when she came to the USA. Her family came here because both of her parents wanted her and her siblings to have a good, bright future and a good education. When she thinks of her

because there are many extremist people who rely on the name of Islam to commit foolish actions to destroy the truth and beauty of Islam. However, in reality, Islam is a religion of peace and of solidarity. She believes that one day the rest of the world will realize that not all Muslims are terrorists and they will stop judging an entire people by the actions of a few people.

What Ramatoulaye wants and believes for the Earth is that one day every country will stop spending billions of dollars on war and weapons; instead money will go for healing from the wounds of wars and for healing the planet and bringing about peace.

Ramatoulaye dreams that one day she can go to one of the best colleges in the U.S. and study aviation to become an Air Traffic Controller. Her dream is to return to Guinea and to help improve transportation so that people will recognize the potential of her country and come to live there and build Guinea a positive future.

where she lived for four years. She moved to the U.S. in 2015 after she met President Obama while she was still living in Malaysia. She can speak Rohingya Mala, Tamil, Indian and English. Rujina loves to dance, cook and shop. She started cooking when she was thirteen years old. She misses all of her best friends and her family that she left behind. She also misses all of the mango trees in her county.

Rujina believes that having her close friends around her will bring her more fun and happiness. She believes that her family and friends can be together again. Rujina dreams of becoming a Reviewing Officer which means she would be of great help to refugees and she would assist them in reaching safety.

Rujina has had many experiences in her life that have made her into a strong young woman. She has lived in shelters and has had to take care of herself at a very young age, living far away from her family and her village. She will try her best to reach her dreams.

Rujina Bibi Mojullah was born in Myanmar, Moni village. She moved to Bangladesh for six months when she was ten years old because she was waiting for the time when she could go to Malaysia. She arrived in Malaysia in 2011,

Sahra Hirsi is a young Muslim woman who was born in Somalia and grew up in Ethiopia with her stepmother and stepsiblings. She is sixteen years old. She speaks Somali and English. At the age of eleven, she moved to the United States to

live with her father and step-siblings. Her father wanted her to have a good education and a safe life because in Somalia people are dying because of the civil war and the drought and it was not safe there.

Sahra misses her mother and her friends and her old teachers. She wishes one day Somalia will be free and livable. She also misses the view of the sunset in the desert, though now she also loves the snow and the cold of the United States. She believes that loving and caring for each other could protect the earth. Sahra's dream is to complete her higher education for social justice and for being a lawyer, to fight the injustices against the women and girls in her country.

Salina Biswa was born in Nepal. She lived in Nepal for eleven years and then moved to the USA. She can speak Nepal, Hindi and English. She loves to play soccer, badminton and run cross country. She likes to cook for her family. Her family tells her to chase her dreams. She loves to learn new things and new experiences. She loves to dance her cultural dances. She wants to travel the world and she wants to help homeless people. Salina wants to visit Nepal again, and see her family and friends. She also wants to graduate high school and get her degree.

One day she wants to graduate from the University of Washington and become a teacher. She loves to play music on her iPhone, to play with her little sister, and to go shopping and buy new clothes. She also loves to go out with her friends and watch movies. Salina loves her culture's food like *momo*, *sambusa* and *achaar*. She likes to sing with her family and she loves to swim in the ocean. She also loves sunflowers and roses.

Samsam Hirsi is seventeen years old. She was born in Mogadishu, Somalia. She lived in Ethiopia for seven years; she grew up there. She moved to the USA with her father and her stepmom. By the time she was eleven, she could speak three languages; Somali, Arabic, and English. She is now learning Spanish. Samsam has hobbies like dancing, reading, and she loves running. She also hopes to become a model or actress because she likes fashion. She is Muslim and she is proud to be Muslim, she is grateful for it. Samsam believes that she can do anything or be anyone in this world no matter how hard or easy. She knows that tomorrow depends on her. In the future she hopes to have a successful life. Samsam thinks that the people on this earth should hold each other's hands to have peace and they should care for their Mother, the Earth.

Shafi Mohamed Osman was born in Somalia. He came to the U.S. when he was sixteen years old. He and his family came to the U.S. for peace because they are from a place where people were killing each other and taking money from people. They lived in a refugee camp in Kenya, Kakuma, for seven years. The camp was not safe. In Kakuma, thieves don't care if it is day or night. They only care about money and killing people. Something he misses about Somalia is the quiet and peaceful places, although he didn't experience that for long. He believes that all living things need peace. In Somalia, there is a saying: *If you keep distracting a bee it will find a way to get out of your distractions and try to find a peaceful place.* He thinks his people can think way more than a bee and look at life in a new way. He thinks people should protect the earth by giving peace and stop changing the beautiful color of the earth into blood. He dreams of a world where everyone can reach their dreams.

Sibhat Gebrekidan was born in Eritrea. He lived in Eritrea for thirteen years and then he moved to Ethiopia illegally. He stayed for four years in the refugee camp called Mayayni. His life there was very difficult because he lived in a group home with eight young adults without his mom and dad. Also, when he was in Eritrea he never washed his clothes because his mom always washed for him. He didn't know how to wash his clothes by hand and if his shoes got old and worn, he didn't know who could buy new shoes for him. When he was underage, he had all the responsibility for himself which is very hard and he always hoped and dreamed of coming to the U.S.

Tewodros Sisay was born in Debre Markos, Ethiopia. He moved to Gonder when he was nine years old. Tewodros then moved by himself to the U.S. in 2017, when he was seventeen years old. He speaks Amharic and English. He dreams of graduating and becoming a basketball player or a Computer Programmer. Therefore, he will try his best to reach his dreams.

He misses his country's food because *injera* is the best food for him. He especially misses having big family dinners sharing *injera* at the table.

When he was a child, he liked to play soccer, but later changed his attention to basketball.

He is learning English because he wants to speak better and he thinks that when we know another language we have better work opportunities. His country is his soul because he spent all of his life there.

Thang S. Khual was born in Myanmar/Burma, Ngennung. He lived in Tedim for thirteen years then arrived in the U.S. in 2014. His family came to the U.S. to have a better life and education. Thang can speak Tedim and English. He is a Christian and he is proud of it. Thang dreams of graduating from flight school and becoming a professional airline pilot. So, therefore, he will try his best to reach his dreams. He also dreams of going back to his country to see his grandparents.

Thang misses his grandparents and the dinners they had together. He also misses what he was doing in his country to help his grandparents. Whenever he prays, he prays for his grandparents to stay healthy. Thang believes that having dinner together makes more connections with his grandparents and makes more love. He also believes that having dinner can bring families together. Thang hopes that one day he will have dinner again with his grandparents.

Ubah Osman was born in Ethiopia, she came to the USA in June of 2013. She came from a small village with all of her family to have a better life. In Ethiopia in the refugee camp where Ubah and her family lived there were shortages of food and water and the government was not always helpful. Ubah hopes to receive a good education, to graduate from high school, to go to college and become a nurse. She wants to help children who are sick or those who need a better life. She also wants to make her parents and her family proud of her.

Ubah believes that in every country we should learn to live with each other in peace and take care of the earth because it is our only home.

Wasim Azizi is from Afghanistan, country of blood, which is always fighting. He was born in Kabul. Wasim is seventeen; he was sixteen when he came to the USA. His dad used to work for the US Army, and because of that, his family was always in danger. He misses the fresh fruit and the vegetables in Kabul. Everything that grows there is natural and unpasteurized. Wasim speaks eight languages: Dari, Pashto, Irani, Pakistani, Hindi, Urdu, Russian, and English. He believes people should be together and grow everything naturally, but now in most of the places where things grow, chemicals are used.

Wasim dreams of a world where fighting will be stopped. In his country there are many beautiful places, but because of the fighting nobody can live there, or because of the fighting they have damaged or broken the beauty of that place and made fearful places of bloodshed, so everyone has to move away.

Zahid Ortiz was born in El Progresso Yoro, Honduras. He moved to the USA in 2014. He arrived in Seattle on July 10th at SeaTac Airport. He feels good in the USA because this country gives you opportunities for going to school and for having a better life. Zahid's dream is to have a job as a mechanic and work for Boeing and to have his own house. What he really misses about his homeland is Christmas with family, food and fireworks.

Zulalureman Ebro grew up in a small city, Bale Robe in Ethiopia. He lived there for fifteen years. He speaks Oromo and a little English. Robe is the capital city of Bale, and has many natural resources. Zulalureman was nine years old when his dad brought him for the first time to school. Bale Robe was a peaceful place, until many protests began happening against the government. He remembers when he was in eighth grade he joined the protest while at school, but in his middle school if you spoke about protests they would expel you.

Zulalureman remembers one day when everyone asked political questions which they were not allowed to do, and when the students received no answers, they protested by burning school property which brought the police. Then Oromo people were beaten and put in jail.

One day his dad and his dad's friends saw a Diversity Lottery in the Internet House. They applied and after that his dad won the lottery and went to the USA. After several years of working on the case to bring his family, his dad succeeded and many in the family came to the USA on May 13, 2016. Zulalureman left his friends, his country, his cousins, his neighbors, and his dogs behind. He hopes he will see his beautiful country and his friends who are still in Ethiopia. His dream is to become a basketball player or to work in Microsoft. Zula dreams of a world where fighting is stopped between governments, and his Oromo people have the freedom and human rights they deserve.

For over 15 years **Carrie Stradley** has dedicated her career to the empowerment of youth as an English Language Learning teacher. Passionate about guiding students through the gauntlet of the English language in order to find their own strong voice and move confidently into their chosen futures, she's thankful for the opportunity to understand the world through the eyes of the immigrant and refugee youth she serves every day.

A National Board Certified Teacher, Carrie has worked in various capacities over the years as a teacher leader and learner. Getting to know the communities of her students and their families has been the highlight of her career. In her free time, Carrie often stares longingly at a framed map of the world in her dining room, and feels it is necessary to keep her passport up-to-date and at hand at all times. When not in the classroom, she delights in raising her two daughters, Isa and Nico, and hopes to instill in them a love of travel, a heart that seeks adventure, and the courage to be strong in their identities.

Merna Ann Hecht is a published poet and essayist, and a nationally known storyteller. She is a recipient of numerous grants and awards including a 2016 King County 4 Culture Individual Artist Grant, a Jack Straw Writers Award and a 2008 National Storytelling Network Brimstone Award for Applied Storytelling. Through this storytelling award, she co-created a poetry/storytelling program at BRIDGES: A Center for Grieving Children in Tacoma, WA. Based on that experience, and her work with young refugees and immigrants, her writing and teaching focus on bringing creative arts to settings for young people who have experienced trauma and loss.

Merna also teaches Arts, Humanities and Social Justice Courses as a part-time lecturer for the University of WA, Tacoma. She is an avid organic gardener who lives on a blueberry farm on Vashon Island. While she loves to stay on the land and tend to her family's flower and vegetable gardens, she would like to work first hand with refugees who are caught in the terrible bind of closed borders and seemingly permanent homelessness. In times of deep concern about human rights and basic human needs lacking for many worldwide, the Stories of Arrival poets inspire her with their spirit of hope and their will and actions toward peacemaking.

Index of the Poets and Artists

Index of the Poets and Artists

CPSIA information can be obtained
at www.ICGtesting.com
Printed in the USA
BVHW020245090119
537371BV00001B/2/P

9 781633 980686